# HEARTWORK

"*HeartWork* paints a picture of a great need today. There are so many people in this world that are broken and hurting, and in desperate need of a glimpse of hope. They want to change their stories, but first they just need to know that it's possible. This book can be that encouragement! *HeartWork* is full of powerful, life-changing points that are equally insightful and practical. Using real stories of real people along with the power of Scripture, Rick and Kelly have written a book that can help you walk out the changed life."

— **Stormy Swann**
Founding Pastor, Faith Christian Family Church

"There is so much power in belief! In believing that God is for us. In understanding that He is on our side. In knowing that God is always present and able to help us through our darkest moments. In *HeartWork*, Rick and Kelly have done an amazing job helping us all to believe in the God of more than enough!

Is *your* heart broken and bitter? Or do you know someone who desperately needs to change their story? Let *HeartWork* introduce you—or them—to the Master Story-Changer!"

— **Steve Smotherman**
Senior Pastor, Legacy Church

"What an amazing book! *HeartWork* is filled with both Biblical stories and real-life stories of struggle, pain, and victory. There is a battle for our hearts, a tug-of-war taking place between God and Satan on a daily basis. Rick and Kelly masterfully guide you through an understanding of God's heart, His desire for our hearts to be changed, and a game plan to make those heart changes permanent. The exercises kick-starting every three chapters are practical yet challenging. If you desire for God to change your story, *HeartWork* is the book for you!"

— **Mike Baskett**
Minister, OpenDoor Church

# HEARTWORK

### How God Can Mend Your Heart
### and Change Your Story

## RICK BURKE AND KELLY S. RIGGS

HeartWork Ministries

For information, please contact:

Kelly S. Riggs
104 N. 67th Street
Broken Arrow, OK 74014


Cover design by samia grafics & Melinda Prescott
Edited by Kristina L. Booker, PhD & LeAnn Gerst

Printed in the United States of America.
First edition 2016.

ISBN-13: 978-0-9845245-2-5 (print)
ISBN-13: 978-0-9845245-3-2 (e-book)

www.HeartWorkMinistry.com

## PERMISSIONS

*Dedicated to those whose lives have been changed
by Jesus, the Master Story-Changer.*

## RICK BURKE

This book has been a journey unto itself that has involved many, many hours of conversation and discussion and study. I am grateful to Kelly, my close friend and confidante, for his hard work and for his heart. You are truly an inspiration!

To the staff and people of Cedar Point Church, I am immensely thankful. We have journeyed together and sacrificed together for ten years now to make Cedar Point a story-changing church. In so many ways—from your personal triumphs to your direct encouragement—you have helped make this book a reality.

I also want to thank three men who have been long-time mentors to me—Steve and Troy Smotherman, and Stormy Swann. You have been steadfast as friends and encouragers, and I appreciate you very much.

Also, I want to give special thanks to David Swann, a very special mentor who gave me the opportunity to serve as a youth pastor at his congregation. I held that position for 17 years, and I grew tremendously under your leadership. Thank you for your willingness to let me grow under your direction. I'm sure it wasn't always easy!

Finally, thanks to my incredible family for their support through the years, especially my wife, Tina. Many times she has set her dreams aside so that I might pursue mine. She has often endured the pain of my shortcomings. I love her with all of my heart, and I am grateful that she never gave up on me.

## KELLY RIGGS

In many ways, I think the best part of writing this book was that it forced Rick and I to spend many, many hours in deep, often introspective, conversation. As we worked through the book's development, those discussions were instrumental in helping me to more completely understand the transformative nature of walking with Jesus. I know very, very few individuals who possess a heart for God's work like Rick does. I am so thankful to have been able to call him my friend for over 35 years.

My chief sounding board throughout the entire writing process was my wife, Rhonda. There are simply no words even remotely adequate to describe how much she has influenced me, or how much I needed that influence! For three-and-a-half decades she has been the glue that has held me together as I have learned how to love as Christ loved. Her encouragement is written all over the pages of *HeartWork*. I love you!

# CONTENTS

# FOREWORD

I am so happy that you're investing time to improve your understanding of how we were made to live—from the inside out! The greatest advancements in our lives have always proceeded from our hearts! Love, encouragement, and courage—these are all traits that we value, and they all originate from within.

Rick Burke, my friend of nearly thirty years, is exactly that kind of person—a man who lives from the inside out. We met in the 80s and we worked together in ministry for over seventeen years. During that time, I found him to be the most relational person I've ever encountered; literally, every aspect of his life revolved around other people!

In the early years of our relationship, we served together in a non-profit ministry, and Rick's focus was on our teenagers. Although the kids could be a lot of fun, they also tended to be a lot of work as well!

One Sunday evening I received a call from two people from our congregation who were employed by Wal-Mart. They happened to be working there that evening, and they had quite a story to tell.

It seems the teens from our church had been engaged in a "treasure hunt," and one of the "treasures" they were attempting to collect was a picture of themselves, together with another teen, in a baby bed. Somehow, they had learned that the one place you could easily find a baby bed for a photo opportunity just happened to be the local Wal-Mart store!

So, on this particular Sunday evening, the Wal-Mart store is full of our teens, who are trying to squeeze two-at-a-time into a baby bed for a picture. Which would be bad enough, but, to make things worse, they are racing through the store, dodging customers left and right, and jumping into these beds as though they might be trampolines instead of baby beds!

Unfortunately, what had started out as a fun activity had managed to turn into a public relations disaster with Wal-Mart—and the manager, as you might imagine, was *not* happy. The police were called, the parents were called, and the whole outing became a major fiasco.

Not one to let a teaching opportunity pass by, I decided the following week that we should address this serious miscalculation as a church staff and learn a valuable lesson. I offered to take the lead and tell the story to everyone, but Rick chose to be the bearer of the bad news.

As he shared the details of the evening's shenanigans, Rick took complete responsibility for the kids' behavior, but he told the story with so much humor that the staff was laughing hysterically, to the point that tears were running down our faces! In the end, as I had hoped, we all learned a valuable lesson, although it came at Rick's expense. He completely shouldered the blame for the poor judgment.

As we began to unwind and turn our attention to other matters, Rick's assistant spoke up. She asked if she might add a short comment to the story, to which I agreed.

The entire tale, she said, was completely accurate. However, Rick had left out one critical detail. "What was that?" I asked.

That one important detail was that she, not Rick, had organized the teens' treasure hunt. She, not Rick, had been the one to encourage the kids to use the Wal-Mart baby beds as props, and, although she appreciated his willingness to suffer ridicule and correction on her behalf, she could not possibly allow Rick to fall on his sword for her. She then apologized to the staff for her lack of maturity and poor judgment.

The room fell silent as the reality of what had just occurred sunk in.

Only an uncommon person with an uncommon spirit is able to stand and accept criticism and judgment rightly deserved by someone else.

I share this story because I think it is important for you to know the kind of man who has contributed to this book. You are going to learn some vital realities about God and His ability to mend your heart; thoughts that have been captured by my uncommon friend, Rick Burke, and his long-time friend and co-author, Kelly Riggs.

Enjoy!

**— David Swann**
Pastor, Faith Christian Family Fellowship

"Glory in his holy name;
*let the hearts of those who seek the Lord rejoice.*
Look to the Lord and his strength;
seek his face always."

**Psalm 105:4-5**

*"Search me, God, and know my heart;*
test me and know my anxious thoughts."

**Psalm 139:23**

You can change your life's story.

Actually, to be more accurate, *God* can change your life's story. No matter where you are now, no matter what your past looks like, no matter what obstacles lie in the way—God can change your story!

First, He will need to mend your heart.

Proverbs 27:19 says, "As water reflects the face, so one's <u>life</u> reflects the <u>heart</u>." This implies that your heart and your life are dependent upon one another.

This book is about linking together those two very important ideas—the ability of God to mend your heart, and, as a result, His ability to radically change your life's story. It is a book that is intended to be transforming; to create radical, positive change in your life rather than producing a short-term, temporary fix.

It is about *healing*, not just feeling better.

Throughout the book, we will share real stories of real lives that have gone off the rails in some way. If you have never experienced the darker sides of life—alcohol, drugs, crime, prison, and worse— some of the stories will boggle your mind. On the other hand, if you have suffered through anger and bitterness and despair, you will find great comfort in knowing that God can mend anyone's heart.

Yes, He can change *anyone's* story, including yours.

Know that none of the people you will read about here would claim that changing their story was free of challenges. None would suggest that scars from the past don't exist, or that life is now perfect and easy. In fact, the temptations of life never go away because the enemy—although already defeated—never gives up. The apostle Peter warned, "Watch out for your great enemy, the devil. He prowls around like a roaring lion, looking for someone to devour."[1]

Inspired by Scripture, and encouraged by the many illustrations of God's grace-filled power of transformation, here is how we have outlined the book to speak directly into your life:

In Section I, we explain why your heart is at war.

In Section II, we discuss how your heart determines the course of your life.

In Section III, we show you how God can, and will, heal your heart.

In Section IV, we detail how God changes your story.

In Section V, we reveal four powerful ways that your heart is a reflection of God.

Finally, in Section VI, we share "God's Instructions" for being saved and living the way God intends.

This main part of the book contains 67 short chapters, each of which can be read in just a few minutes. At the end of every three chapters we have created *HeartWork* exercises that we think you will find to be very helpful, and we encourage you to stop and reflect on them.

Most importantly, before you begin reading, please stop and complete the first *HeartWork* exercise before chapter 1. It will be very important in helping you frame the book for your own personal life, and provide an important reference point for you when you have finished reading.

**Join us as we show you how God can powerfully change *your* story.**

---

[1] 1 Peter 5:8

# PART I

# A HEART AT WAR

"Put on all of God's armor so that you will be able
to stand firm against all strategies of the devil.
For we are not fighting against flesh-and-blood enemies,
but against evil rulers and authorities of the unseen world,
against mighty powers in this dark world,
and against evil spirits in the heavenly places."

**Ephesians 6:11-12 (NLT)**

"Have a heart that never hardens, and a temper
that never tires, and a touch that never hurts."

**Charles Dickens**

# HeartWork Exercise No. 1

**W**hat words would you use to describe your life currently?

For example, would you describe yourself as hurting, or broken, or neglected? Do you feel that something is missing in your life? Would you choose words like "empty" or "lonely," or would you choose more positive words like "joyful" or "blessed" or "loved?"

**Whatever your current situation, think about the words you would choose to describe your story right now**—both the good parts of life *and* the not-so-good parts.

Write those words down below.

Now, write several words or phrases that would describe the story **you would like to be living**. Who would it include? What relationships would it restore? What pains would be erased? Take your time in writing your future story as you imagine what God will do in your life.

# CHAPTER 1

## NO LONGER AN OUTSIDER

"Anyone here who believes what I am saying right now and aligns
himself with the Father, who has in fact put me in charge,
has at this very moment the real, lasting life and
**is no longer condemned to be an outsider.**"

**John 5:24 (MSG)**

**P**eople aren't perfect.

You've probably noticed.

Your family. Your friends. People at work. The many different
people that life puts in your path.

They are all flawed.

It stands to reason, doesn't it? Since they aren't perfect, then by
definition they have a flaw or two. Maybe several.

The truth is that it's pretty easy to see the flaws in others. On the
other hand, we're not always aware of our own personal flaws. We
may not see them, or maybe we just lack the courage to confront
them as we stumble through life from one disaster to the next.

In contrast, there are some people that are far too aware of their
flaws. They feel an enormous burden that arises from the way they
perceive those flaws. Sometimes, they consider themselves to be
*fatally* flawed. Beyond repair. They sense that their flaws are simply
too significant, or too numerous, to overcome—that life's deck is
stacked against them.

They often feel like life's outsiders, living outside and looking in
on everyone else.

> *My parents divorced when I was two. My mother had custody of
> me, while my brother was raised by my father.*
>
> *My mother passed away when I was 12 years old in a tragic car
> accident. This was the first major tragedy I had to endure at a
> very young age. I lost my world that day and nothing would ever
> be the same.*

*By the time I was 14 years old, I started drowning my pain in alcohol.*

*When I was 16, I had my first child, but my father asked me to leave home with my daughter. So we did. Life only became harder.*

*Then, I was 18 and living on my own, and I gave birth to my second daughter. And I married their father.*

*One night while I was at work, the phone rang. It was my husband. He said that our daughter wasn't breathing and that I needed to come home immediately. By the time I arrived home, it was too late. She was gone. I buried her ten days later—on my 19th birthday.*

*Nine months later, my husband was arrested, and eventually convicted, for the first-degree murder of our child. He was sentenced to life in prison. Again, my world was demolished. My baby was taken away from me, and I had been married to the man who had taken her away.*

*My reality was shattered. I remember asking God why he would give me this angel only to take her from me so soon and in such a tragic way. My life was in shambles. That was my rock bottom.*

*Or so I thought.*

*Years passed. My father moved to Asia because he could no longer deal with the pain of my brother's continued drug abuse. I was all alone. However, he decided to come home when my brother was to be released from prison. By this time, I was an adult with three amazing daughters.*

*Although my father was elated that my brother was coming home, he did not realize that his little boy was no longer the same person that he used to know. Upon his release, he continued with his excessive drug use.*

*Eight months later, my father was dead. I spent the last ten days of his life in a hospital room begging God to give me a little more time with him. Then, just like that, he was gone forever. I wasn't sure how I would overcome the intense, crip-*

*pling pain of losing him, or how life could possibly continue without him.*

**Excerpt from Jena's story**

Are you reeling emotionally just from reading that story?

Or perhaps it sounds far too familiar.

For some, it is difficult to comprehend the extreme pain that often exists in people's lives. But it is far more common than we like to think. Every single day, people experience loss and despair, even violence. They wonder if things can *ever* be normal again. They wonder *how* things could ever be different.

But they can be. Yes. Without question. Things can be different!

That's what this book is about. This book is written to encourage you and assure you that you don't have to just let life happen to you. Your story can change. Your heart can mend. No matter how deep the wounds are, and no matter how much pain you've experienced—things can be different.

You don't have to be an outsider.

# CHAPTER 2

# ARE YOU HIDING?

"For all have sinned and fall short of the glory of God."

**Romans 3:23**

**W**hen people feel like outsiders, they tend to think they are all alone.

They might think they are just unlucky, or maybe they just drew the short straw. They look around them and feel that very few people, if any, are burdened with the same kinds of baggage they are carrying around.

Is that you? Has your life sent you burrowing into a deep, dark hole?

Well, you're not alone, not by a long shot.

The reality is that people are never perfect. Not even close.

What that means is that, in the real world—where people are not perfect—even so-called "normal" people have baggage. We all have *some* baggage in our lives regardless of our background, our upbringing, or our circumstances.

Actually, "normal" isn't defined so much by social status, income, or possessions as it is by the way we compare ourselves to others. The way we look at a very small snapshot of someone else's life and decide they must not have any problems. They must be "normal."

Despite what we may perceive, people from absolutely every imaginable circumstance can wind up down a flood-swollen creek in a leaky boat with no paddle.

And, in that sense, *everyone* is an outsider.

Right about now, that may sound crazy. Your life, like Jena's, may feel like one giant disaster, and you can't imagine what someone else could possibly have in common with you. The reality is that many people are very good at hiding.

Are you hiding the pain in your life? Are you pretending life is perfect, but it's really not?

Here is another of the many stories we will share with you as we go along. It's from a couple named Mandy and Jerry, and it illustrates how "normal" lives can be very misleading:

> In the fall of 2012, the story for our family didn't look very promising. We were in the process of remodeling a new home, had good jobs, and lots of material things, but that is where the positives stopped. However, anyone around us thought we were happy and successful.

They certainly *looked* happy and successful. A new home. Good jobs. Lots of material things. Everyone around them thought they were doing well.

Except they really weren't. They were just hiding. Though it may have looked like a picture-perfect story, Mandy tells us that, "addiction, idolatry, pride, and very worldly goals were poisoning us."

The truth is that everyone suffers some measure of damage and loss in their lives. Some may endure and experience much more—and much worse—than others, but regardless of degree, somewhere along the way all of us have wished we could change our stories.

Pretending things are fine won't make them fine.

# FIRST, FORGIVE YOURSELF

*"Forgetting what is behind and staring toward what is ahead, I press on toward the goal...."*

**Philippians 3:13-14**

$\mathbf{Y}$es, the truth is that we are all flawed.

So, ironically, your flaws only make you like the rest of us.

This means that, quite often, the first step in mending your heart and changing your story is to *quit punishing yourself.* You must first forgive yourself and then realize that your past does not have to dictate your future.

Did you catch that?

Go back and read that last sentence again. You cannot fail to see how incredibly important it is to forgive yourself. Yes, you may have made mistakes—big mistakes. Yes, you may need to ask forgiveness from others, but you will never mend your heart if you continue to dwell on the failures of your past.

Circumstances and decisions have brought you here, but things can change.

God can, *and will,* change your story.

We want to help you see what has happened in your life to this point and what needs to happen differently going forward. Changing your story will require you to let God mend your heart. Then, you will need to change your direction, change your circumstances, and look carefully at your influences.

As we will discover, it will require you to find the courage to forgive yourself.

# HeartWork Exercise No. 2

As you begin reading this book, do you know someone else who is struggling in life? Someone who, at this very moment, feels lost or hopeless or bitter? What they need more than anything in life is to encounter someone who can show them what *real* love looks like.

You could be that someone. You could provide a word of encouragement or a gesture of kindness. You could be the person that prompts them to move in a new direction.

*You might play a role in helping someone else's story to change.*

Write down their names below, and make a point to reach out to them in the next few days.

# CHAPTER 4

# THE PROMISE OF ANOTHER DAY

"The Lord our God is merciful and forgiving, even though
we have rebelled against him."

**Daniel 9:9**

The novel *Les Miserables* is a very, very, *very* long story.

It has been adapted to film, television, and radio, and made into one of the world's most popular and successful Broadway musicals.[2]

It is a story of hopelessness, mercy, and second chances.

Written by Victor Hugo in 1862, *Les Miserables* focuses on the life of a fictional character named Jean Valjean during the early 1800s in France. It is a story about—and, in many cases, it is Hugo's direct commentary on—the injustices of life. It is a story that exposes the faults of mankind in our dealings with one another. It is a story that explores popular perceptions of what is right and what is wrong.

Here is how Hugo himself described his magnificent book:

> "The book which the reader has before him at this moment is, from one end to the other, in its entirety and details...a progress from evil to good, from injustice to justice, from falsehood to truth, from night to day, from appetite to conscience, from corruption to life; from bestiality to duty, from hell to heaven, from nothingness to God."

From beginning to end, Hugo intended the book to illustrate the plight of the outsider.[3] In the story, Valjean, one of those "outsiders,"

---

[2] The book is approximately 1,500 pages long. It's been made into a movie on several occasions. The most recent version (2012) starred Hugh Jackman, Russell Crowe, and Anne Hathaway. My (Kelly) favorite adaptation is the 1998 film starring Liam Neeson, Geoffrey Rush, and Uma Thurman. For many years, it was the classic movie our family watched at Christmas.

is imprisoned for stealing bread and eventually spends 19 years of his life in prison—five years for stealing, and fourteen additional years for his escape attempts.

Finally, released from prison, Valjean's yellow passport does nothing more than brand him as an ex-convict. Unable to find work or a place to sleep, he eventually finds food and rest with a charitable bishop and his wife. Hardened and bitter with few prospects for changing his life, Valjean decides to slip away during the night, taking the family's silver with him.

He is quickly apprehended. He is returned to the bishop's home, along with the pilfered silver, to face the music. However, much to the surprise of everyone present (especially his wife), the bishop claims Valjean didn't steal the silver at all:

> "Ah! here you are!" he exclaimed, looking at Jean Valjean. "I am glad to see you. Well, but how is this? I gave you the candlesticks too, which are of silver like the rest, and for which you can certainly get two hundred francs. Why did you not carry them away with your forks and spoons?" Jean Valjean opened his eyes wide, and stared at the venerable Bishop with an expression which no human tongue can render any account of. "Monseigneur," said the brigadier of gendarmes, "so what this man said is true, then? We came across him. He was walking like a man who is running away. We stopped him to look into the matter. He had this silver—" "And he told you," interposed the Bishop with a smile, "that it had been given to him by a kind old fellow of a priest with whom he had passed

---

[3] In a commentary on *Les Miserables*, Susanne Alleyn writes: "And finally—the phrase "les misérables," which has a whole range of subtly shaded meanings in French, is much better translated into English as "the dispossessed" or even as **"the outsiders"**—which can describe every major character in the novel in one way or another—than simply as "the miserable ones" / "the wretched ones." *Historical Fiction Ebooks*. "No, It's Not Actually the French Revolution: Les Miserables and History." January 27, 2013. Retrieved from http://hfebooks .com/no-its-not-actually-the-french-revolution-les-miserables-and-history-by-susanne-alleyn/

the night? I see how the matter stands. And you have brought him back here? It is a mistake."

> "This is what the Lord Almighty said: 'Administer true justice; show mercy and compassion to one another.'"
>
> **Zechariah 7: 9**

"In that case," replied the brigadier, "we can let him go?" "Certainly," replied the Bishop. The gendarmes released Jean Valjean, who recoiled. "Is it true that I am to be released?" he said, in an almost inarticulate voice, and as though he were talking in his sleep. "Yes, thou art released; dost thou not understand?" said one of the gendarmes. "My friend," resumed the Bishop, "before you go, here are your candlesticks. Take them." He stepped to the chimney-piece, took the two silver candlesticks, and brought them to Jean Valjean. The two women looked on without uttering a word, without a gesture, without a look which could disconcert the Bishop. Jean Valjean was trembling in every limb. He took the two candlesticks mechanically, and with a bewildered air. "Now," said the Bishop, "go in peace. By the way, when you return, my friend, it is not necessary to pass through the garden. You can always enter and depart through the street door. It is never fastened with anything but a latch, either by day or by night."

Then, turning to the gendarmes: "You may retire, gentlemen." The gendarmes retired. Jean Valjean was like a man on the point of fainting. The Bishop drew near to him, and said in a low voice: "Do not forget, never forget, that you have promised to use this money in becoming an honest man." Jean Valjean, who had no recollection of ever having promised anything, remained speechless.[4]

For perhaps the first time in his life, Valjean experienced mercy. It was the promise of a new day, one without scorn, imprisonment, or hopelessness.

---

[4] Victor Hugo, *Les Miserables*. Signet. Kindle Edition (locations 2315-2321).

But Valjean still had a choice to make. "You have promised to use this money in becoming an honest man," the bishop told him, and Valjean could have easily squandered his newly acquired.

But he didn't.

Despite his past, his bitterness, and his many flaws, Valjean went on to be a decent, kind, and generous man. Through the charity of another, his heart was mended and his story changed.

**No, it's not a true story.** But we have witnessed many, many broken lives that have been transformed by the charity of another, and we know that God can mend your heart and change your story in very much the same way.

God's mercy gives the hope and promise of another day.

# CHAPTER 5

# THE MASTER STORY-CHANGER

"As [John the Baptist] preached, he said, 'The real action comes next: The star in this drama, to whom I'm a mere stagehand, will change your life.'"

**Mark 1:7 (MSG)**

Each of us is unique, so each of us has a unique story.

Our genuine hope is that your current story is one of fullness and joy and that you are sharing it with others as a source of encouragement. However, in our experience, that often isn't the case. Rather than joy or hope or fulfillment, many people's stories are marred with disappointment, disillusionment, and despair.

Of course, if Jesus has already stepped into your path, you already know there is good news! You already know that the ultimate message of the gospel[5] is that Jesus can change your story!

Yes, Jesus is the Master Story-Changer. If you have not yet come to know Him personally, our hope is that this book will be the start of that journey.

> "Therefore, if anyone is in Christ, the new creation has come: The old has gone, the new is here!"
>
> **2 Corinthians 5:17**

The *good news* is that regardless of your past or your present, and regardless of your deeds or misdeeds, God sent His Son to earth to give you the opportunity to rewrite your story: no matter how bad things may be right now; no matter how unworthy you may feel; no matter how bitter you may have become. If your story isn't what you want it to be, God stands ready, willing, and able to help you change it.

In the first century, Saul of Tarsus was a man on a mission. And his mission was simple—rid the world of Christians.

---

[5] The word "gospel" literally means "good news."

He was an intensely devout man who zealously defended Judaism. He had, in fact, committed his very life to destroying the sect of 'The Way,' people who had little regard, so it appeared, for the Law of Moses on which his life and heritage were built.[6]

In Acts 22, Saul (now Paul, after his conversion to Christ) shared his story with a crowd in Jerusalem.

> "I am a Jew, born in Tarsus of Cilicia, but brought up in this city. I studied under Gamaliel and was thoroughly trained in the law of our ancestors. I was just as zealous for God as any of you are today. I persecuted the followers of this Way to their death, arresting both men and women and throwing them into prison, as the high priest and all the Council can themselves testify. I even obtained letters from them to their associates in Damascus, and went there to bring these people as prisoners to Jerusalem to be punished."

**Acts 22:3-5**

This well-educated, religious man—the eventual author of over a dozen books in the New Testament, and founder of many churches in Europe and Asia Minor—was guilty of beating, imprisoning, and killing believers. In a letter to the church at Galatia, he said, "For you have heard of my *previous way of life* in Judaism, how intensely I persecuted the church of God and tried to destroy it" (Galatians 1:13).

That was before Jesus changed his life.

On a dusty road to Damascus, as he embarked on yet another campaign to flog and jail the followers of The Way, the Lord appeared to Saul in a blinding light:

> "'Saul! Saul! Why do you persecute me?'
>
> '*Who are you, Lord?*'
>
> 'I am Jesus of Nazareth, whom you are persecuting.'"

**Acts 22:7-8**

---

[6] "The Way" was used as a label for early Christians in Acts 9:2, 19:9, 19:23, 22:4, 24:14, and 24:42.

An encounter with Jesus can be like that. You don't see it coming. It can happen when you least expect it. You don't have time to think about your response. Instead, you're suddenly confronted with a yes-or-no decision: will you continue down your current path, or will you choose to change your story?

The challenge is to have the courage to hear the help that is offered and to be honest with yourself because the encounter may not sound like help at all to you. To you, it may sound like judgment, criticism, or even condemnation. Changing your story requires you to be honest with yourself, and that's not always easy!

Then again, your face-to-face with Jesus may not be nearly so dramatic. It might sound like an invitation to go to church, or a word of encouragement, or a phone call from a friend.

One thing is certain: God will call. Think back in your own life. There is little doubt that God has placed someone in your path who has confronted you with a truth about your life. Perhaps they have offered encouragement or help.

Did you miss it?

The problem is that when our lives are broken, and we are drowning in pain and despair and self-pity, the hurt is overwhelming. As a result, we defend our behavior. We justify our poor choices. We may not see that helping hand.

We fail to recognize God's calling.

For Saul, the answer was never in doubt. In fact, the most amazing thing about this whole story is Saul's *immediate* response: *"What shall I do, Lord?"*

How will you respond to God's call?

# CHAPTER 6

# HOW WILL GOD CONFRONT YOU?

*"...they hid from the LORD God among the trees of the garden.
But the LORD God called to the man, 'Where are you?'"*

**Genesis 3:8-9**

$\mathbf{Y}$es, God will step into your path.

His appearance might be big, bold, and dramatic, like it was with Saul.

It might be a gentle whisper, like it was with Elijah.

After years of preaching to the nation of Israel, Elijah, the great prophet of God, found himself completely alone and in fear for his life. The Bible says that he went out into the desert, sat down under a tree, and prayed for death!

God appeared to Elijah and asked him what he was doing. Defeated and disillusioned, Elijah broke down.

> "'Your people have rejected you and killed all the prophets,'" he told God. 'I am the only one left,' he said, 'and now they are trying to kill me, too. I have had enough. Take my life....'"

God knew that Elijah desperately needed Him. He knew he needed to be encouraged, strengthened, and reassured.

> "The LORD said, 'Go out and stand on the mountain in the presence of the LORD, for the LORD is about to pass by.' Then a great and powerful wind tore the mountains apart and shattered the rocks before the LORD, but the LORD was not in the wind. After the wind there was an earthquake, but the LORD was not in the earthquake. After the earthquake came a fire, but the LORD was not in the fire. And after the fire came a gentle whisper. When Elijah

heard it, he pulled his cloak over his face and went out and stood at the mouth of the cave."

**1 Kings 19:11-13**

Boldly, like Saul, or gently, like Elijah.

One way or another, God will step into your path. You *will* have an encounter with Jesus, the Story-Changer. It might be at that point in your life when you just don't know where else to turn or what else you can do.

Are you listening?

Jesus is calling, and He wants to change *your* story.

# HeartWork Exercise No. 3

Think back in your life—have you encountered God somewhere along the way? Do you think that somewhere in the past God has placed someone in your path?

If so, did you recognize the value of that moment, or did you work harder to defend your actions than to consider the help?

Write down the names of anyone who may have encouraged you or been there to listen when you needed it most.

Now, consider this: gratitude is a powerful emotion. Truly, gratitude has the power to heal your heart. For each of the names you wrote down, take a few minutes to jot down a word of thanks to that person. Or send them a text or an email message. If you're up to it, pick up the phone and call.

Sharing your heart will begin the healing process.

# CHAPTER 7

# THE SOIL, THE SEED, AND THE HARVEST

"Do not be deceived: God cannot be mocked.
A man reaps what he sows."

**Galatians 6:7**

$T$he 'Parable of the Sower' is a story about sowing and reaping.[7]

Jesus tells of a farmer who sows seed on different types of ground. As the seed is sown, each type of ground produces different results.

Some seed, Jesus says, falls beside the road and is simply eaten by the birds. The result? Complete failure.

Other seed falls on rocky ground with very little soil, and the plants soon wither and die for lack of roots. The result? At first, there is hope, but as the plants wither, it is quickly followed by disappointment.

Still other seed falls on thorny ground. Although the plants begin to grow, the thorns grow up as well and choke out the plants before they can produce grain. The result? There is great expectation, but again, disappointment follows.

Still, there is some seed, Jesus explains, that falls on fertile soil, and the result is a bumper crop, a crop that is as much as "a hundred times what was sown!"[8] The result? Hope, then expectation, and then great joy as the plants are harvested.

To anyone who has planted seeds, this sounds like common sense. So, what is the point?

Like all the parables that Jesus taught, there is a deeper meaning to the story. The story has spiritual significance, one that His disciples didn't quite understand.

---

[7] You can find this parable in Matthew 13:1-15, Mark 4:1-12, and Luke 8:4-10.
[8] See Mark 4:20.

So Jesus explains:

"The seed is the Word of God.

Those along the path are the ones who hear, and then the devil comes and takes away the word from their hearts, so that they may not believe and be saved.

Those on the rocky ground are the ones who receive the word with joy when they hear it, but they have no root. They believe for a while, but in the time of testing they fall away.

The seed that fell among thorns stands for those who hear, but as they go on their way they are choked by life's worries, riches, and pleasures, and they do not mature.

But the seed on good soil stand for those with a *noble and good heart,* who hear the word, retain it, and by persevering produce a crop."

**Luke 8:11-15**

Jesus used this very simple story to teach us something incredibly profound. The lesson is that the different types of ground in the parable represent different conditions of the people who hear the Good News—the story-changing message—and the different ways in which the seed responds to each of those soils.

Most importantly, Jesus teaches that the "soil" where God sows His word is **your heart.**

Your heart may need attention. It may need *serious* attention. Don't be discouraged. It may take some work, but the stones and thorns can be removed from your heart.

If you haven't already, you need to hear the gospel message.

# CHAPTER 8

# THE GOSPEL MESSAGE

"For God so loved the world that he gave his one and only Son, that whoever believes in him shall not perish but have eternal life."

**John 3:16**

$T$he real problem in the world is sin.

It is as simple as that. Sin is what Satan uses to manipulate you, control you, and convince you that everything is fine.

> "Everyone who sins is breaking God's law, for all sin is contrary to the law of God."
>
> **1 John 3:4 (NLT)**

However, in the bigger picture, sin is just one piece of the puzzle. Sin is just another word for disobedience. For disobedience to occur, there must be a command or statute of some kind that creates a rule or standard to be followed. In addition, there must be a real temptation to ignore the command and choose to do as you please.

"Each person is tempted when they are dragged away by their own evil desire and enticed. Then, after desire has conceived, it gives birth to sin; and sin, when it is full-grown, gives birth to death."

**James 1:14-15**

To summarize: Our selfish desires produce temptation. Temptation, if pursued, results in disobedience, which is sin. And sadly, sin produces death—a spiritual separation from God which means that you are on your own, sentenced to live forever with the consequences of your actions.

The important thing to remember is that when God created you, He blessed you with the ability to make your own choices. He doesn't force you to follow Him in obedience. Instead, He offers you a choice; one that is first described in the Old Testament as a choice between life and prosperity, and death and destruction.[9]

Jesus echoed that choice during His ministry here on earth:

> "Very truly I tell you, whoever hears my word and believes him who sent me has eternal life and will not be judged, but has crossed over from death to life."

**John 5:24**

Anyone who has ever been separated from someone they truly love can understand the severity of separation. And that is what sin does—it separates us from our Creator, the one who loves us more than anything. This separation, destructive as it is, was remedied in the resurrection of Jesus:

> "This includes you who were once far away from God. **You were his enemies, separated from him by your evil thoughts and actions.** Yet now he has reconciled you to himself through the death of Christ in his physical body. As a result, he has brought you into his own presence, and you are holy and blameless as you stand before him without a single fault.
>
> But you must continue to believe this truth and stand firmly in it. Don't drift away from **the assurance you received when you heard the Good News.**"

**Colossians 1:21-23 (NLT)**

The Good News—the gospel message—is that God himself has provided a solution to our sin and death problem. Through the sacrifice of His own son, Jesus, He paid off your debts—provided that you "continue to believe this truth *and* stand firmly in it."

In other words, if you choose to accept Jesus as both Savior *and* King, repenting of your sinful behavior and choosing instead to walk in obedience to His ways, the blood of Jesus continually cleanses your sins![10]

---

[9] See Deuteronomy 30:15.
[10] See 1 John 1:7.

If you are searching for life's meaning, this is it. God loves you. He loves you so much that He provided a way out of your sin and death problem.

He only asks that you love Him in return.

> "Whoever has my commands and keeps them is the one who loves me. The one who loves me will be loved by my Father, and I too will love them and show myself to them."

> **John 14:21**

Will you do so?

# CHAPTER 9

# DAYS WITHOUT MEANING

"Remember, O God, that my life is but a breath; my eyes will never see happiness again…I despise my life; I would not live forever. Let me alone; my days have no meaning."

**Job 7:7,16**

**P**ride, anger, and bitterness: too often, these emotions are the thorns that prevent the seed of God's Word from taking root in our lives. As in any good garden, the preparation of the soil is absolutely critical to the quality of the harvest.

Stop for a moment and search deep inside your own heart. Have the worries of life, or insecurity, or fear, or anger, or some other powerful emotion taken possession of your heart?

Could these thorns prevent the seed of God's Word from taking root?

That is exactly what happened to Jackie. Her 19-year old nephew, Kyle, was gravely injured in a terrible 4-wheeler accident. In a coma and on life support, Kyle was never expected to survive the ordeal. Though people prayed fervently for Kyle's recovery, Jackie's past choked out any hope she might have had.

> *But rather than accept that verdict, the in-laws and friends (who had now all gathered at the hospital) joined hands and began a prayer-filled vigil with the Lord. To not believe a doctor's verdict and turn to prayer, instead, seemed like denial to me. Twenty years prior, I had prayed (more like begged) God to heal my Mom of cancer. He did not. Instead, he allowed her to die and did nothing. I hadn't worshiped in a church since. What was the point? I mean, God was all fine and good when things were going OK. But when you really need him, he does nothing. Plus, I was uncomfortable in churches, feeling judgment and condemnation.*

**Excerpt from Jackie's story**

These very powerful emotions may seem very familiar to you, maybe even now.

It is the intensity of these feelings—anger and bitterness—that choke out any opportunity for God to work in your life. These are very powerful emotions that Satan uses to wreck your story, and he will seize on any and every opportunity to use them to defeat you.

In the coming chapters, we are going to show you how God steps into people's paths, heals their hearts, and changes their stories. We are going to show you how to rebuild the walls of your life and create genuine happiness for you and your family.

First, you need to see that your heart is much more than the soil where the Word of God is planted.

Your heart is also a battleground, and you are at war.

# HeartWork Exercise No. 4

William Churchill famously said, "Success is not final; **failure is not fatal**: it is the courage to continue that counts."

To continue—to allow God's Word to find root in your heart and produce a crop of joy, peace, and love—means that you need to identify and confront the "thorns" that threaten to choke out the joy in your life.

What are those thorns in your life? What are the issues that are pressing against your heart?

Be brutally honest with yourself. Write them below.

Bookmark this page and come back to it often as you progress through the book. These are some of the most important issues that you will have to resolve in order to mend your heart and change your story.

# CHAPTER 10

# THE MEANS TO DEFEND YOUR HEART

> "Put on the full armor of God, so that you can take your stand
> against the devil's schemes. For our struggle is not against
> flesh and blood, but against the rulers, against the authorities,
> against the powers of this dark world and against the
> spiritual forces of evil in the heavenly realms."
>
> **Ephesians 6:11-12**

The first thing you *must* understand is that your heart is a battle-ground.

Quite simply, you are under attack.

Have you ever thought about what that looks like?

It looks like conflict, betrayal, and heartbreak. It feels like disappointment and pain. However, once you figure out the source of that attack, you can take steps to defend yourself and the process of mending your heart can begin.

The source of these attacks is your *enemy*. He is Satan, the father of lies.[11]

Each day, Satan has one singular objective: he is out to defeat you. He does not play fair. He will use the people you love or people you don't know. He does not care who is damaged or destroyed in the process, and he will not relent until your heart is taken captive—or until you defeat him.

Yes, the battle that is being waged is a very real one. There is a winner, and there is a loser. There are injuries. There is very real pain. And the battleground where this tremendous battle is taking place is your *heart*.

However, unlike any other battle you know of, the outcome is already determined. The Scripture says very clearly that victory is assured!

---

[11] See John 8:44.

In James 4:7, the Bible says, "Resist the devil, and he will flee from you." *Resist* him. In the Greek language, the word "resist" (*anthistemi*) literally means "to set yourself against something; to *actively oppose* something."

Yes, just as we are called to defend ourselves in real, physical battle, we must *actively* defend ourselves in this spiritual battle.

Paul, in Ephesians 6, describes the "armor" that God provides for this fight. It is an armor that consists of six different items: a helmet, a shield, a breastplate, a belt, shoes, and a sword. It is very important to note that Paul *twice* says that we should put on the "full armor" of God. To fight without any one piece means that you are more susceptible to defeat.

> The helmet of salvation.
>
> The breastplate of righteousness.
>
> The belt of truth.
>
> Your feet fitted with the readiness of the gospel.
>
> The shield of faith.
>
> And the sword of the Spirit.

A helmet to protect your head. A breastplate to protect your vital organs. With your shield of faith, Paul says, you can "extinguish all the flaming arrows of the evil one" (Ephesians 6:16).

Notice that God's armor includes an offensive weapon, a sword. While the breastplate and the shield are crucial to defending your most vital organ—your heart—the sword is necessary to *actively oppose* Satan. You need it to fight back.

God will prepare you for the battle.

# CHAPTER 11

## GUARDING YOUR HEART

"Though an army besiege me, my heart will not fear; though war break out against me, even then I will be confident."

**Proverbs 27:3**

When Rick was living in New Mexico, he had a good friend named Donald who had retired from the Air Force. For years, Donald would swing by Rick's house at 6:30 a.m. to pick him up, and the two would head off to Cannon Air Force Base for an early morning workout.

Getting in and out of the base was really pretty routine. Both men had passes, which they showed at the gate, and after a cursory glance the guard would wave them through. Rick and Donald would head to the weight room, complete a workout, then head back out the way they came and give the guards a wave as they left.

Routine.

Nothing to it.

One morning, things changed. Rick and Donald arrived at the gate as usual, but rather than a quick look at their passes, the guard asked them to park the car and enter the guardhouse.

Inside the guardhouse, there was a line of people waiting. In a serious but respectful manner, the guard asked each man for his ID. Both were asked to verify the make and model of the vehicle in which they had entered. There was a form to fill out.

It was a fairly lengthy process just to go to the gym, but the change in procedure became permanent.

*That day was September 12, 2001.*

Clearly, the events of the previous day had created a heightened awareness of security at military installations around the globe. Those events created changes in security procedure and made everyone much more guarded against threats that might exist.

From that day on, access to the base would only be given with certainty that whoever was entering would not be a threat to the base, its personnel, or its mission.

You could likely share stories about how your life changed on 9/11 as well.

It is interesting that it wasn't until the tragedy of 9/11 that we as a nation became very serious about security and access.

Consider what God says about the safety and security of your heart:

> "My child, pay attention to what I say. Listen carefully to my words. Don't lose sight of them. Let them penetrate deep into your heart, for they bring life to those who find them, and healing to their whole body. *Guard your heart* above all else, for it determines the course of your life."

> **Proverbs 4:20-23 (NLT)**

*Guard your heart.*

Your breastplate of righteousness is, in fact, the last line of defense to your heart. The implication is that being in a "right relationship" with God (righteousness) *is* that line of defense.

So, would you say that your diligence in guarding your heart is at a pre-9/11 status or a post-9/11 status? Are you hypervigilant in guarding your heart?

If not, what would it take to become serious about protecting your heart?

# CHAPTER 12

## A FIGHT TO THE DEATH

"The cords of death entangled me, the anguish of the grave came over me; I was overcome by distress and sorrow."

**Psalm 116:3**

**W**e seriously underestimate the threat that Satan poses to our hearts.

That's why the stories in this book are so common.

Unless, and until, something disastrous happens, we may not be paying close enough attention to those threats. We may not be adequately prepared to defend this critical battleground.

Satan will not fail to attack. He will use any weapon necessary to win, including deceit. He will find your point of vulnerability and attempt to exploit it. He will not lose interest. He will not give up.

A clever enemy, he will not only create pain and despair, but he will also help convince you that God himself is to blame.

Think about this: Why is it that when people suffer their first thought is often to blame God? Many people will, in fact, walk away from God, believing Him to be the enemy for *allowing* things to happen while Satan sits off to the side and quietly celebrates both your pain *and* your decision to blame God.

You simply cannot afford to underestimate the value of your heart and the ferocity with which Satan will fight to gain control of that valuable ground.

> "*Take to heart* all the words I have solemnly declared to you this day, so that you may command your children to obey carefully all the words of this law. They are not just idle words for you—they are your life."

**Deuteronomy 32: 46-47**

You *must* guard your heart. If you don't, Satan will lead you down a path that—on the surface—looks wonderful. He will convince you to dismiss the punitive and limiting "rules of religion" and follow your own way. What Satan won't mention is that decisions made selfishly ultimately end in death and destruction.

> "The mind governed by the flesh is death, but the mind governed by the Spirit is life and peace."

> **Romans 8:6**

Satan is prepared to fight to the very end.

Are you?

The idea of "doing battle" may be a bit hard to swallow, but, thankfully, this battle does not require physical conflict. However, the pain and scarring from *emotional* conflict are often just as bad, if not worse, than any physical scars.

The "good news" is that God has provided the means for victory in your fight to defend your heart. Go back and look at the "armor" that God has provided, the tools of spiritual warfare. Notice the protective elements of that armor:

- **A helmet of salvation**: Accepting Christ, being saved, and becoming a part of the kingdom of God provide protection for the head where your thinking occurs. Paul says, "So, from now on we regard no one from a worldly point of view."[12] He is speaking of those who belong to Christ, and he says that our salvation changes the way we think about others.

- **A breastplate of righteousness**: Right living (righteous-ness) serves to protect our hearts in the same way that a breastplate will protect you physically from a potential "death blow." To wander into the world and continue living in ways that are opposed to God (unrighteousness) will create vulnerability to your most vital organ.

- **A shield of faith**: God is saying that our faith creates the first line of defense for our hearts in the same way that a shield is the first line of protection against

---

[12] See 2 Corinthians 5:16.

a physical blow to the body. What is faith exactly? In Scripture, Hebrews 11:6 says, "Anyone who comes to Him must believe that he exists, and that he rewards those that earnestly seek Him." Faith, then, is an unwavering belief that God truly exists; a belief causes the believer to *earnestly* seek Him.

So, are you wearing the "helmet" of salvation? Are you saved? Our prayer is that you have already responded to God's call, but if not, please go to chapter 66 and read **"God's Instructions for Being Saved."**

Also, the breastplate of righteousness is a very important piece of armor! It is the last line of protection for your heart. What is righteousness? Simply defined, righteousness is "right living." But right living isn't a big book of rules—a set of do's and don'ts. Instead, it is a set of principles and ideals for treating others the way God intends. You'll find a helpful summary in chapter 67: **"God's Instructions for Right Living."**

For this exercise, write down why you believe God exists.

CHAPTER 13

# THE FAITH OF A FIGHTER

"Have I not commanded you? Be strong and courageous.
Do not be afraid; do not be discouraged, for the Lord
your God will be with you wherever you go."

**Joshua 1:9**

Oone of the most familiar stories in the Bible is most likely the story
of David and Goliath: the shepherd boy, David, and his slingshot
versus the soldier, Goliath, a hulking giant of a man—a trained, pro-
fessional, killing machine.

> "Goliath stood and shouted to the ranks of Israel,
> 'Why do you come out and line up for battle? Am I
> not a Philistine, and are you not the servants of Saul?
> Choose a man and let him come down to me. If he is
> able to fight and kill me, we will become your sub-
> jects; but if I overcome him and kill him, you will
> become our subjects and serve us.'"

**1 Samuel 17:8-9**

The Bible records that King Saul and his soldiers were not merely
worried; they were terrified. This one man caused the entire army of
Israel to flee in fear.[13]

David's reaction, however, was radically different.

> "David said to Saul, 'Let no one *lose heart* on account
> of this Philistine; your servant will go and fight him.'"

**1 Samuel 17:32**

Pretty brash talk from a lowly shepherd, don't you think?

David was not yet the warrior he would later become. He certainly wasn't a fighter; he was barely old enough to be considered a man!
As King Saul observes, "You are not able to go out against this Phil-

---

[13] See 1 Samuel 17:11, 24.

istine and fight him; *you are only a young man*, and he has been a warrior from his youth."[14]

Goliath was not just any warrior, by the way. Standing over nine feet tall, Goliath towered over ordinary men. He carried a spear that may have weighed as much as David. Well, that's a bit of an exaggeration, but you get the idea. Goliath made grown men *cower* in fear.

Not David. No, David didn't fear Goliath at all. Instead, full of courage and brimming with the confidence that comes only from an unwavering faith in God, David actually calls out Goliath:

> "'You come against me with sword and spear and javelin, but I come against you in the name of the Lord Almighty, the God of the armies of Israel, whom you have defied. This day the Lord will deliver you into my hands, and I'll strike you down and cut off your head.'"

**1 Samuel 17:45-46a**

Stop for a moment and think about this unlikely scene. On the Israelite side, hardened fighting men are shrinking in fear, and this young boy with no armor, no weapons, and clearly no good sense claims that he will not only defeat Goliath, but he will do so in the most humiliating fashion imaginable: *with a slingshot.*

Most likely, David's "arrogance" set off a good laugh among the Philistine army. Goliath, however, is not amused.

> "[Goliath] looked David over and saw that he was little more than a boy, glowing with health and handsome, and he despised him. He said to David, 'Am I a dog, that you come at me with sticks?' And the Philistine cursed David by his gods. 'Come here,' he said, 'and I'll give your flesh to the birds and the wild animals!'"

**1 Samuel 17:42-44**

David brings only his five stones against Goliath. Now, on top of everything, Goliath is viciously angry. What chance do you think David has in a one-on-one battle?

---

[14] See 1 Samuel 17:33.

Actually, it's exactly the same chance you have in a battle with Satan.

Your victory is assured!

Yes, in the battle that is critical to mending your heart and changing your story, your victory is certain.

> "What, then, shall we say in response to these things?
> If God is for us, who can be against us?"
>
> **Romans 8:31**

# CHAPTER 14

# THE HEART OF A LION

> "Be strong and courageous. Do not be afraid or terrified because of them, for the Lord your God goes with you; he will never leave you nor forsake you."

> **Deuteronomy 31:6**

**H**ow many times have YOU been there?

You are alone, anxious, and fearful. Life seems to pile up like a snow drift against your front door, trapping you inside. Your hope has left you and the only thing you find in its place is fear.

That is exactly what it is like to *lose heart*. It means that circumstances overwhelm you to the point of fear and despair and hopelessness.

Did you notice that when David spoke of Goliath, he said, "Let no one lose heart"?

He didn't say, "Don't be *afraid*." Instead, he said it this way: "Let no one *lose heart*."

This is the beginning of a very powerful lesson.

You see, the English word "courage" has its origins in the Latin root word "cor." And, as it turns out, the word "cor" is Latin for "heart." In other words, having courage literally means that someone has "heart."

For example, in the Middle Ages, Richard I, the twelfth-century king of England, was known as *Richard the Lionhearted*. He was the king with the heart of a lion, known far and wide as a warrior with great courage.

Actually, courage and heart have always been joined together in the English language. This is certainly true in the original sense of the two words "courage" and "heart." Long before the common English meaning of the word "courage" was used to describe a person's bravery, it simply meant "inner strength."[15]

The ideas of heart and courage are also linked together in the Scriptures. Long after his exploits with Goliath, David becomes engaged in a conflict with his own son, Absalom, who foolishly considered attacking his own father. Here is the counsel Absalom receives from one of his advisors:

> "'If David should attack first, then even the bravest soldier, **whose heart is like the heart of a lion**, will melt with fear, for all Israel knows that your father is a fighter and that those with him are brave.'"

> **2 Samuel 17:10**

*The bravest soldier's heart is like a lion.*

The point is that your heart is not only a battleground, but it is also where your courage resides. When your courage falters or fails, it is because your heart has grown weak or melted with fear.

In order to change your story, you will need the courage of David. Have you lost heart? Have you lost the will to fight?

There is no need to worry. God is more than happy to provide.

> "Be strong and courageous. Do not be afraid or terrified because of them, for the Lord your God goes with you; he will never leave you nor forsake you."
>
> **Deuteronomy 31:6**

---

[15] Etymology of the word "heart." Circa 1300, from Old French *corage* (12th century., Modern French *courage*) "heart, innermost feelings; temper," from Vulgar Latin *coraticum* (source of Italian *coraggio*, Spanish *coraje*), from Latin *cor* "heart," from PIE root *\*kerd-* (1) "heart," which remains a common metaphor for inner strength. *Online Etymology Dictionary*. Retrieved from http://www.etymonline.com/index.php?term=courage.

# CHAPTER 15

# THE BATTLE IS THE LORD'S

"You armed me with strength for battle; you humbled
my adversaries before me."

**Psalm 118:39**

The toughest parts of life often occur when we wind up in circumstances we never see coming.

Looking at your life right now, do you sometimes wonder, "how in the world did I get here?"

Looking back, it may be that you ignored the warning signs. Maybe you just closed your eyes to the path you were on. In reality, it is the bad choices we make that lead to undesirable circumstances and the negative consequences that accompany them.

Regardless of how you may have gotten there, getting out of a bad situation requires a decision to be courageous. You have to decide to fight, not in the literal sense of physical confrontation, but in the sense of finding the courage to make different choices and change your circumstances.

You must decide to confront your circumstances.

This is exactly what David did. He *chose* to confront his enemy, an enemy that caused even Israel's best fighters to quake in fear.

David never wavered, and he never doubted.

Where did that courage come from? As we mentioned, to the casual observer this was clearly no contest. It should have been over before it started. Without God, the story of David and Goliath would be a forgotten footnote in ancient history, a lesson only in the folly of youth.

The truth is that the outcome was never in doubt.

> "David said to the Philistine, 'You come against me
> with sword and spear and javelin, but I come against

you in the name of the Lord Almighty, the God of the armies of Israel, whom you have defied. This day the Lord will deliver you into my hands, and I'll strike you down and cut off your head. This very day I will give the carcasses of the Philistine army to the birds and the wild animals, and the whole world will know that there is a God in Israel. All those gathered here will know that it is not by sword or spear that the Lord saves; **for the battle is the Lord's**, and he will give all of you into our hands.'"

**1 Samuel 17:45-47**

Clearly, David's confidence didn't come from an analysis of his fighting capabilities or from a belief in his own strength. Notice also that his confidence wasn't limited by the difficulty of his circumstances.

Instead, his confidence, his *faith,* was in God.

In our own lives, when we are confronted by the enemy, we must make a conscious decision: will we fight, or will we let our fears dictate our responses?

Again, you know that when we use the term "fight," we're not talking about physical conflict (like David and Goliath); instead, we're talking about the battle for your heart: the battle to defeat Satan and conquer your fears.

In the absence of *confidence*, the decision to fight courageously will be difficult, even impossible.

> "Now faith is confidence in what we hope for and assurance about what we do not see."
>
> **Hebrews 11:1**

What, or who, are the "giants" in your life? What seemingly unmovable challenges do you have to overcome? Insecurity? Fear? Financial issues? Dependency?

How will you change the circumstances of where you are right now? How will you change directions?

The only way is to place your confidence in God and allow Him to change your story. This is how you find the courage to confront the obstacles and barriers in your life. It is how you find the courage to make new choices.

Remember, the battle is the Lord's.

As your heart mends, your courage to resist will continue to grow.

> "This is the *confidence* we have in approaching God: that if we ask anything according to his will, he hears us. And if we know that he hears us—whatever we ask—we know that we have what we asked of him."
>
> **1 John 5:14-15**

# HeartWork Exercise No. 6

As we discussed, the Latin word "cor" is the root of the English word "courage." It is also the root of the word "encouragement," which means that when you encourage others, you are giving them heart! You are giving them the capacity to overcome adversity!

What this means is that encouraging others can be among the most effective things you can do to help them. The Scripture says:

> "Let us think of ways to motivate one another to acts of love and good works. And let us not neglect our meeting together, as some people do, **but encourage one another**, especially now that the day of his return is drawing near."

**Hebrews 10:24-25 (NLT)**

There are many, many ways to encourage others, both in words and in actions, and God knows how powerful it is for us to do so. In *HeartWork Exercise No. 3,* we asked you to express your gratitude to those people who had encouraged you somewhere along the way. You probably remember exactly how good it felt to be encouraged.

Now, we would like to ask you to take a moment and write down the names of at least three people you know and decide to encourage them in the same way.

What do you say? Try this:

"I just want to take a moment and tell you how much I appreciate you."

Also, tell them why. And watch their courage swell because you've given them some of *your* heart.

# CHAPTER 16

# THE WAY SATAN WORKS

"Be on your guard; stand firm in the faith;
be courageous; be strong."

**1 Corinthians 16:13**

$T$he third chapter of the first book in the Bible (Genesis) is the first time we see Satan at work.

In every circumstance, Satan will seek out any weakness or vulnerability, and he will do everything he can to convince you that he is not the enemy. Instead, he whispers in your ear that the problem is God.

Shortly after creation, Adam and Eve are enjoying the paradise prepared for them by God, and everything is…well…perfect! God has created a beautiful garden for them to enjoy, and there is really only one command from God that they have to consider.

God had said, "You are free to eat from any tree in the garden; but you must not eat from the tree of the knowledge of good and evil, for when you eat from it you will certainly die."[16]

So, the Garden of Eden seems like a pretty nice arrangement, doesn't it? Everything is provided. The food is plentiful and free. There aren't a bunch of rules and regulations. Just eat, drink, and enjoy.

Well, you can eat from every tree but *one*.

As we have learned, when Satan sets his sights on your heart, you won't always see him coming. Eve didn't. Neither, as it turned out, did Adam, who was no help at all.

> "Now the serpent was more crafty than any of the
> wild animals the Lord God had made. He said to the

---

[16] See Genesis 2:16-17.

woman, 'Did God really say, "You must not eat from any tree in the garden?"'

The woman said to the serpent, 'We may eat fruit from the trees in the garden, but God did say, "You must not eat fruit from the tree that is in the middle of the garden, and you must not touch it, or you will die."'

'You will not certainly die,' the serpent said to the woman. 'For God knows that when you eat from it your eyes will be opened, and you will be like God, knowing good and evil."'

**Genesis 3:1-4**

The serpent was *crafty*.

That word means "subtle" or "sly." That's exactly what Satan is. Here is our interpretation of what he says: "No, that's not *really* going to happen. You won't die. God just doesn't want you to think for yourself. He's trying to control you. Actually, once you know what God knows, things will really be great!"

This apparently had just enough truth, just enough allure, to make Eve disobey God.

Look at what Scripture says:

"When the woman saw that the fruit of the tree was good for food and pleasing to the eye, and also desirable for gaining wisdom, she took some and ate it. She also gave some to her husband, who was with her, and he ate it."

**Genesis 3:6**

Eve "saw" that the fruit was "good." But God had already said that eating the fruit from *that* tree was forbidden. So, by definition, it couldn't be good! Anything and everything else was fine, but *that* tree was off-limits.

Through subtle manipulation, Satan changed Eve's perspective. She became convinced that something God had prohibited was actually fine.

Sound familiar?

Then, just to make herself feel better, Eve further justified her choice to disobey God's command by convincing herself she will be wiser for having eaten the fruit: *good-looking fruit, great for food, AND wisdom, to boot?* What's not to like?

So she disobeyed.

The consequences? Both she and Adam would face death, exactly as God had said, both physically and spiritually. They would be expelled from the Garden of Eden. They would be forced to work the ground (to toil) in order to eat rather than simply gathering fruit from the trees.

Sadly, this is our story; this is what we do. We allow ourselves to be manipulated. We choose short-term pleasure over long-term wisdom. We live selfishly.

When we decide not to follow God's direction—when we decide not to do things God's way—we demonstrate that we don't really trust His way. When we choose our own path, we place our trust in ourselves rather than God.

If we would only trust God to determine what is good for our lives and not allow Satan to deceive us, things would go so much more smoothly. Instead, we convince ourselves that we deserve to be happy, so, in our minds, the decision isn't *really* wrong. We convince ourselves that we deserve to have what others have, so the decision isn't *really* bad.

Satan is counting on that.

# CHAPTER 17

# At Your Weakest Point

*"But as for me, I almost lost my footing. My feet were slipping,*
*and I was almost gone."*

**Psalm 73:2**

Life is often a challenge on the *best* of days, isn't it?

We all have so many responsibilities: at home, at work, to our kids, with our parents. There's more than enough to make even the average day a trial.

Even so, there are times when life seems to go completely off track. On those days, life can be pretty overwhelming.

Stop and take a look at your life. Are you overwhelmed? Maybe you are, and maybe you aren't. Regardless, one thing is for sure: Satan is always looking for a way into your heart, and 'overwhelmed' is a context he can easily work with.

He will wait until you're exhausted, frazzled, or distracted. Sometimes he just has to wait until you're comfortable. But he will wait until just the right moment, when you least expect it.

He will pry apart your most cherished relationships. He will drive a wedge between you and God. He will try to convince you that God is the problem. He will, in fact, do anything and everything possible to make things look completely hopeless.

That's when you will want to throw in the towel. That's when your courage will be spent, and you won't really see the point of trying.

Stacey wasn't quite to that point, but she was close.

> *Three years ago tonight my life, our life, our marriage was forever changed.*
>
> *Adultery, pride, anger, bitterness and brokenness had our marriage chained up. The following week I didn't know who to call*

*or where to go...I picked up the phone and called Cedar Point Church. Through the sobs, I was finally able to speak clearly enough for Sunny to understand what I was saying. She got a message to [Rick] and [he] immediately called me back.*

*I sat in the parking lot of my work telling [Rick] the story about my broken marriage. [He] cried with me and told me [he] would do what [he] could to help. I walked back into church the next Sunday after being gone for two years. I never felt so welcomed and loved as I did that day walking through those doors. From that day forward, my life and my marriage were forever changed.*

*Jesus Christ, guidance and support from you, church counseling, Celebrate Recovery, and many supportive people helped us on this journey.*

*That phone call changed our story. We are forever grateful!*

### Excerpt from Stacey's story

She didn't know who to call or where to go, but she picked up the phone just in time.

When Satan springs his traps, the first thing he tries to convince you is that you don't need help. In fact, when you start trying to convince yourself that everything is OK, that is a pretty good sign that you *do* need help:

*"I don't want to bother anyone with my problems."*

*"I'm too embarrassed to tell anyone."*

*"People will think I'm weak."*

*"I can work this out on my own. It will get better."*

These are big red flags that need to be heeded. And the very best way to know the truth is to share your challenges with someone who truly loves you, *and has nothing to gain or lose from telling you the truth.*

A **critical step** in your life being "forever changed" is the courage to reach out and ask for help, to be vulnerable, and to share your pain and bitterness with someone who will listen.

Just remember that Satan will want you to believe that it's too late and that you're too far gone. You're not. God has never given up on you.

If God hasn't given up on you, it is *never* too late!

> "What, then, shall we say in response to these things?
> If God is for us, who can be against us?"
>
> **Romans 8:31**

# CHAPTER 18

# HIDING GOD IN YOUR HEART

> "I have hidden your word in my heart that I might
> not sin against you."
> **Psalm 119:11**

**"Y**ou get to pick your choices. You don't, however, get to pick your consequences."

A good friend made this statement in a Bible class a few years ago. His name is Jim Roberts. Although he retired long ago, Jim works closely with men just released from prison. He is a remarkable individual with an incredible knack for helping people see the good in who they are and where they are, regardless of their circumstances.

His observation is remarkable in its simplicity. When you boil it all down, life really is all about the decisions we make. As Jim suggests, you get to pick your choices. However, you should think long and hard about those choices because the *consequences*—what happens as a result of your choices—may not be what you signed up for.

The most important choices we make usually occur when Satan confronts us with temptation.

Consider how he confronted Jesus in the wilderness:

> "For forty days and forty nights [Jesus] fasted and became very hungry.
>
> During that time the devil came and said to him, 'If you are the Son of God, tell these stones to become loaves of bread.'
>
> But Jesus told him, 'No! The Scriptures say, "People do not live by bread alone, but by every word that comes from the mouth of God."'
>
> Then the devil took him to the holy city, Jerusalem, to the highest point of the Temple, and said, 'If you are

the Son of God, jump off! For the Scriptures say, "He will order his angels to protect you. And they will hold you up with their hands so you won't even hurt your foot on a stone.'"

Jesus responded, 'The Scriptures also say, "You must not test the Lord your God."'

Next the devil took him to the peak of a very high mountain and showed him all the kingdoms of the world and their glory. 'I will give it all to you,' he said, 'if you will kneel down and worship me.'

'Get out of here, Satan,' Jesus told him. 'For the Scriptures say, "You must worship the Lord your God and serve only him."'

Then the devil went away, and angels came and took care of Jesus."

**Matthew 4:1-11 (NLT)**

Have you ever gone a single day without food? Two days? Three?

Could you even imagine 40 days without eating? Jesus must have been *famished*. So Satan tempted Him to use a miracle to feed Himself.

*Bread? There is so much more to life than bread. There is God.*

Then, because Satan knows that man can be egotistical and proud, he tempted Jesus by suggesting that He prove himself.

*Test God? Not a chance.*

Finally, realizing that Jesus might be tempted to trade away His integrity and His allegiance to God in order to save the people of the world from death, Satan offers to exchange them for a price—to bow down and worship *him* rather than God.

*Seriously? There is only one God, and you're definitely not him. Take a hike.*

It is a dramatic moment, and it is incredibly important. Why? The Bible clearly says that Jesus is able to completely understand our pain and weaknesses since He has been "tempted in every way, just as we are" and "yet he did not sin" (Hebrews 4:15).

How did Jesus overcome those three powerful temptations?

*Go back and read the passage again.*

Notice that in all three cases, Jesus says: "The Scriptures say...."

Jim Roberts asked this powerful question in that same Bible class:

> **"Could you hide enough of God's Word in your heart that you could resist Satan when he comes calling?"**

It's an incredibly powerful question!

When crafty, subtle and clever Satan comes calling, he comes to do battle. The way in which you *actively oppose* him is with the offensive weapon that God supplies, the sword of the Spirit.

That sword, according to Scripture, is "the Word of God."[17]

That is exactly the weapon that Jesus chose to use. Rather than giving in to His personal needs or wants, or pursuing His own selfish ambitions, He relied upon the very words of God to defeat Satan.

Jesus didn't defeat Satan miraculously. He used the power of God's word.

Couldn't you do the same?

Couldn't *you* hide God's words in your heart as a defense?

> "For the **word of God** is alive and active. Sharper than any double-edged sword, it penetrates even to dividing soul and spirit, joints and marrow; it judges the thoughts and attitudes of the heart."
>
> **Hebrews 4:12**

---

[17] See Ephesians 6:17.

# HEARTWORK EXERCISE NO. 7

The example that Jesus provided in Matthew 4:1-11 was to **oppose** Satan. Not to simply ignore him or appease him, but to *oppose* him. Jesus didn't compromise, and He didn't negotiate. His answers did not lack clarity or boldness: His answers were the words of God.

"For the Scriptures say...."

There is much to learn in Scripture, but most of us tend to rely on church to provide that knowledge. Hiding God's Word in your heart means spending time in the Word! While there are dozens of ways to approach Bible reading, **starting somewhere is better than never starting at all**.

Here's how you can easily start to acquire knowledge of God:

For practical wisdom about life, read <u>one</u> chapter from Proverbs **every day for one month**. [31 chapters]

To learn about the life of Jesus and His ministry, read <u>two</u> chapters from Mark **each weekend for 8 weeks**. [16 chapters]

*Next:*

To observe David's intense love for God, and to discover more about the character and nature of your Creator, read one chapter from Psalms **every weekday for 6 weeks** [the first 30 chapters]. In Week 7, read through Psalm 119. Read **35 verses at a time for 5 days**. [176 verses]

To understand the early church and the mission trips of Paul, read <u>four</u> chapters from Acts **each weekend** for 7 weeks. [28 chapters]

In four months, you will have a much stronger relationship with God, a much clearer picture of the love that Jesus has for you, and a greater sense of the glory and wisdom of God.

Just as physical exercise makes the body stronger, this "exercise" will make your heart stronger.

# PART II

# THE COURSE OF YOUR LIFE

"I will give them a heart to know me, that I am the Lord.
They will be my people, and I will be their God,
for they will return to me with all their heart."

**Jeremiah 24:7**

"The face is the mirror of the mind, and eyes,
without speaking, confess the secrets of the heart."

**St. Jerome**

# CHAPTER 19

## APPEARANCES CAN BE DECEIVING

"And he who searches our hearts knows the mind of the Spirit,
because the Spirit intercedes for God's people in
accordance with the will of God."

**Romans 8:27**

$Y$our heart is the place where your life's story is being written.

It is also the place where the war for your life's story is being waged.

What you may not realize is that your heart is where God looks first when He sees you. Unlike most of us, God doesn't look at your outward, physical appearance. He doesn't look at your money, your background, or your achievements. He doesn't use any of the things that we tend to rely on to form opinions of people.

To know the *real* you, to know what is really going on in your life, God looks directly at your heart.

It is something that we learn about God from the life of David, even before his famous encounter with Goliath. This story begins when God directs the prophet Samuel to anoint a new king for Israel.

> "Now the Lord said to Samuel, 'You have mourned long enough for Saul. I have rejected him as king of Israel, so fill your flask with olive oil and go to Bethlehem. Find a man named Jesse who lives there, for I have selected one of his sons to be my king.'"

**1 Samuel 16:1 (NLT)**

Israel's very first king, Saul, had failed to obey God and had selfishly pursued his own direction and sought honor for himself. God asked Samuel to go to Bethlehem and seek out the family of Jesse, where he was told he would find the man who would be the new king of Israel.

Samuel did as the Lord instructed. When he arrived at Bethlehem, the elders of the town came out to meet him, but they were somewhat confused about why he had come. "What's wrong?" they asked. "Do you come in peace?"

> "'Yes,' Samuel replied. 'I have come to sacrifice to the Lord. Purify yourselves and come with me to the sacrifice.' Then Samuel performed the purification rite for Jesse and his sons and invited them to the sacrifice, too.
>
> When they arrived, *Samuel took one look at Eliab and thought, 'Surely this is the Lord's anointed!'*"

**1 Samuel 16:5-6 (NLT)**

Of course, when Samuel went looking for Israel's new king, he knew exactly what *he* was looking for: a man that *looked* like a king. A man with physical presence. A commander.

Isn't that what we would be looking for? Aren't we often guilty of making decisions about people based on what we see? Thankfully, however, God isn't distracted by appearance.

The Lord said to Samuel:

> "Don't judge by his appearance or height, for I have rejected [Eliab]. The Lord doesn't see things the way you see them. People judge by outward appearance, **but the Lord looks at the heart.**"

**1 Samuel 16:7 (NLT)**

You see, we might be deceived by a person's appearance, but God is not. The Lord looks right into your heart. He looks there, because that's where the *real* you is found. You may try to hide, but God sees the truth. He sees the *real* you.

It's a good thing, isn't it? Quite often, we actually feel inadequate because of our outward appearance: too tall, too short, too big, too small, not so attractive. On and on we go, creating scorecards for ourselves as we measure against impossible standards we've often made up in our own minds.

No matter how much our culture may value physical appearance, God is much more concerned with what's in your heart.

Thankfully, God doesn't see us as we see ourselves.

As you know, appearances can be very deceiving.

> "Stop judging by mere appearances, but instead judge correctly."
>
> **John 7:24**

# CHAPTER 20

# A HEART HELD CAPTIVE

*"Get rid of all bitterness, rage and anger, brawling and slander, along with every form of malice."*

**Ephesians 4:31**

$Y$es, appearances can be deceiving.

Consider the Biblical story of Simon, the Sorcerer:

> **"A man named Simon had been a sorcerer** there for many years, amazing the people of Samaria and claiming to be someone great. Everyone, from the least to the greatest, often spoke of him as "the Great One—the Power of God." They listened closely to him because for a long time he had astounded them with his magic.
>
> But now the people believed Philip's message of Good News concerning the Kingdom of God and the name of Jesus Christ. As a result, many men and women were baptized. **Then Simon himself believed...."**

**Acts 8:9-13 (NLT)**

For his day, Simon was kind of a big deal. He put on quite a show, and he caused quite a stir! The people in that region called him "the Great One."

When Simon was confronted with the message of Jesus, his heart was touched. Having seen the miracles of God at work in the apostles, Peter and John, Simon decided he wanted it for himself.

> "When Simon saw that the Spirit was given when the apostles laid their hands on people, he offered them money to buy this power. 'Let me have this power, too,' he exclaimed, 'so that when I lay my hands on people, they will receive the Holy Spirit!'"

**Acts 8:18-19 (NLT)**

Simon was a man who thought he could actually *purchase* the gifts of God. One might suspect that Simon was the type of man who was used to getting what he wanted, and that he usually did so using his money. So, he did what we might expect any businessman would do; he offered the apostles money in exchange for the power of the Holy Spirit!

It was, to say the least, an interesting proposition, considering how Peter might have reacted. After all, he was performing miracles!

Although Peter did not respond in the extreme, his reply was certainly quite blunt:

"And the Lord's servant must not quarrel; instead, he must be kind to everyone, able to teach, not resentful. Those who oppose him he must gently instruct, in the hope that God will grant them repentance leading them to a knowledge of the truth, and that **they will come to their senses and escape from the trap of the devil, who has taken them captive to do his will."**

**2 Timothy 2:24-26**

"'Your *heart* is not right before God. Repent of this wickedness and pray to the Lord in the hope that he may forgive you having such a thought in your *heart*. For I see that you are **full of bitterness and captive to sin.'"**

**Acts 8:21-23**

Captive to sin.

Full of bitterness.

For many people, this is what their stories sound like. So, when God looks into your heart, He sees a heart that is bitter and has been taken captive. He sees a heart that is losing the battle!

To change the course of your life is to change the thoughts of your heart. It is to escape captivity.

And, as we have seen, to escape that captivity you have to be willing to "fight."

You see, there is no need to be held captive, because God provides the means to resist, to defend yourself, and to escape.

# CHAPTER 21

## WHAT DOES GOD SEE IN YOU?

"The Lord looks down from heaven and sees the whole human race.
From his throne he observes all who live on the earth."

**Psalm 33:13-14 (NLT)**

So, what does God see in *your* heart?

Does God see humility, compassion, and love?

Does He see arrogance, selfishness, and rebellion?

One of the stories that we want to share with you is from a young man named Andrew. His story, with few exceptions, is extraordinarily sad. In fact, the hurt in his story can be overwhelming at some points.

Read as Andrew describes himself:

> *I had a rebellious spirit and a problem with authority. I was in school, in the fifth grade, when my bad attitude got a good start. I stopped doing anything that anyone tried to make me do, either in school or out. I loved to read and I loved to learn, but I noticed that the school either couldn't teach me anything I didn't know, or wouldn't be patient with me about what I didn't know. I got to where I wouldn't do anything for someone I didn't respect, and the only way to get that respect was to give it to me first. Maybe some of my teachers were the same way, therefore we didn't quite get along.*

Andrew's journey has been a struggle almost from the beginning.

He was born, as he says, into a "happy, Christian family," but things began to go quite wrong very early. Pills. Public intoxication at twelve. A juvenile record. Alcoholism at thirteen. Addiction. Violence. Jail.

There are a dozen factors or more that contributed to Andrew's plight. Although it's not difficult to understand the results, at the root of it all was a heart that rebelled against goodness.

> *I have blamed God for all of this, and bitterness and unforgiveness (sic) has poisoned my heart and mind. Not only did I blame God, but I hated Him. My hate for God spread to hate for Christians and the church itself. There was a time when my anger was so intense that I made up my mind to find reasons for disbelief. I had such an aversion to Christianity that I tried everything I could to convince myself that God didn't even exist. Yet through all the doubt and pain, my answer for dealing with everything was to remain intoxicated.*

Thankfully, as you will soon see, all that changed.

You can read Andrew's entire story at the following website: www.heartworkministry.com/stories. We encourage you to stop and go there and read it now. You will see that God confronted Andrew over and over again. God kept looking deep into his heart, knowing there was goodness there, despite the outward appearance.

Remember, God not only looks at the heart, the Bible tells us that God "*searches* the heart."[18]

We can say what we want, and we can pretend all we want, but the heart reveals exactly who we *really* are. God will search until He finds the man or woman that He created, or until you give up on Him.

What is God seeing in you right now?

> "I the LORD search the heart and test the mind,
> to give every man according to his ways, according
> to the fruit of his deeds."
>
> **Jeremiah 17:9-11 (ESV)**

---

[18] See Romans 8:27.

# HeartWork Exercise No. 8

$T$he things we say tell people a lot about us. The words we use, the manner in which we use them, and the ways in which we deliver them are a reflection of the things that reside in our hearts. A well-known Chinese proverb says, "If you wish to know the mind of a man, listen to his words."

Scripture says it this way:

> "Make a tree good and its fruit will be good, or make a tree bad and its fruit will be bad, for a tree is recognized by its fruit. You brood of vipers, how can you who are evil say anything good? For the mouth speaks what the heart is full of."

**Matthew 12:33-37**

Think about the things that you say to your loved ones. Are your words kind? Are they encouraging? Or are they toxic, or unkind, or discouraging?

In his letter to the Ephesian church, Paul wrote: "Do not let any unwholesome talk come out of your mouths, but only what is helpful for building others up according to their needs, that it may benefit those who listen."[19]

As your heart mends, the words you use should begin to change. In what part of your life do you need to change the way you speak to others?

---

[19] See Ephesians 4:29.

# CHAPTER 22

# A Man After God's Own Heart

"Put me on trial, Lord, and cross-examine me.
Test my motives and my heart."

**Psalm 26:2 (NLT)**

Stop for just a moment and imagine what someone might say about your life and your character that you would consider to be a tremendous compliment.

Here are some thoughts that may come to mind:

*She genuinely cares about people.*

*He has such incredible love for his family.*

*She is a beautiful person on the inside.*

*He would give you the shirt off his back.*

*She goes out of her way to help people in need.*

*You could call him at 3 a.m. and he would gladly help you.*

Who wouldn't be flattered by any of these comments?

But imagine for just a moment if God himself had this to say about *you*:

"I have found David son of Jesse, a man after my own heart...."

**Acts 13:22**

Can you imagine? God's description of David was that he was a man after God's own heart. God looked at David and saw a man whose thoughts were similar to His own, a man who had the love and compassion and goodness that HE possesses!

Isn't that amazing? God looked at David and saw a piece of himself! He saw someone who had the same *motives* and the same perspective. Stop and think what it would be like if God said that about you. Could you imagine God looking at you and seeing a person after His own heart?

We have learned that God looks at the heart, but it's more than that. God doesn't just look at your heart; He looks at the *motives* within your heart.

> "All a man's ways seem innocent to him, but *motives* are weighed by the Lord."

**Proverbs 16:2**

God looks behind the curtain. God doesn't just see *what* you do; He sees *why* you're doing it. In fact, it's interesting to note that the Proverb writer says that the Lord doesn't just *look* at our motives; He **weighs** our motives.

In the original Hebrew language of the Old Testament, those words have an interesting meaning. The Hebrew words say that God is *measuring* or *testing* (Hebrew: *takan*) our *spirits* (Hebrew: *ruwach*).

What that means, in simple language, is that God is looking at the very essence of who we are. The Revised Standard Version of the Bible translates that passage much more closely to the original language when it says: "All the ways of a man are pure in his own eyes, but the LORD *weighs the spirit*" (Proverbs 16:2 RSV).

So, when you consider that God himself would look at your life, your influence, your priorities, your relationships—every aspect of who you are—and determine that YOU are a person after His heart, is there anything more flattering?

Yes, that *would* be unbelievable.

That couldn't possibly be me. No chance. After all, a man or woman after God's own heart would have a soaring faith. She would have a daily Bible devotion and prayer time. He would be a great husband. She would be the perfect mom. They would be loved and admired by all and pillars of the community.

No, you might be thinking, a person after God's own heart would have a life that is very different from mine. I couldn't possibly qualify to be a person after God's own heart. My flaws are simply too numerous.

That is simply not true.

When God looks into your heart, He's not keeping score. He is looking at your motives, the intent of your heart. Despite your flaws, if your heart is pursuing God first and foremost, and you are serving those around you, then you are a person after God's own heart.

Exactly like David.

# CHAPTER 23

# YOU CAN BE THAT SOMEONE, TOO

"My hands have made both heaven and earth; they and everything in them are mine. I, the Lord, have spoken! 'I will bless those who have humble and contrite hearts, who tremble at my word.'"

**Isaiah 66:2 (NLT)**

The truth is that David was a flawed man if there ever was one.

Despite all of his victories and his humble devotion to God, he was, in many ways, a flawed man. In fact, he was surprisingly flawed.

Consider these things from his life:

He had an affair.

He took the life of an innocent man.

His marriage was a mess.

His kids were rebellious.

He got caught up in his pride.

He disobeyed God.

A man after God's own heart?

Oh, yes, David experienced incredible victories, but he suffered gut-wrenching tragedy.

He demonstrated awe-inspiring faith, but was guilty of adultery.

He spared the life of a sinful king bent on taking his life, but sent an innocent man to his death to cover his own sin.

Still, God loved him deeply. You know, maybe you and I *could* be someone after God's own heart after all.

What would it take? What kind of person do you have to be to be a person after God's heart? Clearly, looking at David, you don't have to be perfect. So, what exactly did God see in David? After all, David slept with another man's wife and arranged it so that her husband would be killed in battle. David was so unaware of the extent of his sin that the Lord had to send a man to confront him directly.

How would we describe David?

Foolish. Selfish. Clueless. *A man after God's own heart?*

It hardly seems possible.

Psalm 51 provides us with some clues. David wrote this psalm after God confronted him about his sin.

> "Have mercy on me, O God, according to your unfailing love; according to your great compassion blot out my transgressions.
>
> Wash away all my iniquity and cleanse me from my sin.
>
> For I know my transgressions, and my sin is always before me.
>
> Against you, you only, have I sinned and done what is evil in your sight; so you are right in your verdict and justified when you judge."

**Psalm 51:1-4**

What does God see in David? He sees a man that is flawed, yes, but a man that truly loves the Lord with all of his heart. David has a soft, tender heart, and, when confronted with his guilt, he does not lay the blame elsewhere.

Yes, he is a selfish man, but when confronted with the immensity of his sin, he is completely and wholeheartedly humble before God.

Like Saul on the road to Damascus, he had to be confronted. Like Saul, his humility was immediate.

The truth is that a person with a good heart responds to God's rebuke. He or she is a person who is humble, trusts in God, accepts His call for change.

But, to defeat you, Satan needs you to be cynical, bitter, and hopeless. He needs you to reject God's call and choose your own selfish path.

The question is, how will you respond to God when He confronts you with your sin?

# CHAPTER 24

# TRUSTING GOD COMPLETELY

"The Lord is my strength and shield. **I trust him with all my heart**.
He helps me, and my heart is filled with joy.
I burst out in songs of thanksgiving."

**Psalm 28:7 (NLT)**

On December 15, 2014, a group of people gathered together for another session of *Celebrate Recovery*®.

If you're not familiar with the organization, *Celebrate Recovery*® was created over 20 years ago. It is "a biblical and balanced program that helps us overcome our hurts, hang-ups, and habits," and is based on "the actual words of Jesus rather than psychological theory."[20]

This particular evening, a young woman named Kimberly shared her story with the audience. It is a very sad story; one that is, sadly, all too common. But, praise God, her story ended in triumph. Though the beginning was painful and sad, it ends in victory for one reason. It includes an encounter with Jesus, the Master Story-changer.

Here is a part of that story, in her own words.

> *I kept being invited to Celebrate Recovery, but honestly I wasn't looking for that at the time. So I tried the church.*
>
> *At first, the hellos seemed distant and few, but it wasn't going to matter to me cuz when that Pastor [Rick] spoke he had every bit of my attention. It's like he knew me and understood me... And, guess what? He said he loves me!!*
>
> *Me, a convicted violent offender.*
>
> *Me, an addict.*
>
> *Me, a mother who lost custody of her blessing from Above.*
>
> *After being abandoned, beaten, on the verge of suicide.*

---

[20] For more information, visit www.celebraterecovery.com.

*He loves me.*

*I kept attending the Sunday service and learning more about the bible and some of [the church's] way of doing things. That next fall I attended partnership. This was where I knew I belonged. I signed the partnership agreement with a smile. I then decided to give back and serve my new family that loved and accepted me.*

> "You, God, are my God, earnestly I seek you; I thirst for you, my whole being longs for you, in a dry and parched land where there is no water."
>
> **Psalm 63:1**

*All my dreams came true when I walked down the aisle of my home church, where I felt comfortable and accepted, to face my soon-to-be husband, the man who first showed me unconditional love and acceptance.*

*I continue to grow in my walk with the Lord God and share with people my change. Most people can instantly see that this wild heathen has been transformed. The only one who could possibly heal the broken person I was is My Father God himself. Love living my testimony. And love my church family.*

### Excerpt from Kimberly's Story

Clearly, people make mistakes.

They falter. They fail. They choose poorly.

Sometimes, like Kimberly, they are victims of horrible circumstances.

Think back to David. He chose poorly. He failed miserably. Yet, God still saw him as a man after His own heart! Why? Because, despite his flaws, and despite his weaknesses, David's faith in God never wavered.

Can you be like David? Can you be a man or woman after God's own heart?

Absolutely. If you will respond to your flaws and weaknesses and failures in the same way that David did, the answer is absolutely yes.

# HeartWork Exercise No. 9

Sometimes, when life begins to go wrong, or it just seems empty, our thoughts and attitudes can turn negative. We can go dark and, sometimes, stay there. It is always good to be reminded that you are special and to know that God blessed you with certain talents and abilities.

Take some time to consider your life and who you really are. Write down the complimentary things you think people might say about you, if they knew the *real* you.

# CHAPTER 25

# IS YOUR HEART BROKEN?

"The Lord is close to the brokenhearted and saves those
who are crushed in spirit."

**Psalm 34:18**

The truth is that the only real cure for a broken life is a *broken heart.*

That doesn't sound quite right, does it? A *broken* heart?

No, it doesn't really sound quite right, but it's true nevertheless. A healed heart is one that is actually broken in God's presence. For you to change your story, what you actually need is a *broken* heart.

You may be thinking, "I'm not sure that word means what you think it means."

Have you seen the wonderful film, *Princess Bride?* If so, you recognize that line.[21] Directed by Rob Reiner, it is a post-modern fairy tale that tells the story of Westley and his undying love for the most beautiful woman in the world, Princess Buttercup.

The primary plot line in the story is the kidnapping of Buttercup and Westley's never-ending pursuit to free her from the kidnappers. As Westley gives chase over great distances and numerous obstacles, one of the kidnappers, the Sicilian criminal genius, Vizzini, sets numerous traps for him. Westley overcomes each obstacle and continues to gain ground on the kidnappers.

"*Inconceivable*," Vizzini says over and over, until finally Inigo Montoya, the Spaniard, turns and says, "*You keep using that word. I do not think it means what you think it means.*"

From God's perspective, a broken heart doesn't mean what we think it means. It's actually a good thing. You see, when we speak of

---

[21] The movie *Princess Bride* was written by William Goldman and directed by Rob Reiner. Twentieth Century Fox Film Corporation (1987). For more information, visit http://princessbrideforever.com.

a heart being broken, we usually mean that something has happened that irreparably damaged a very important relationship or that something tragic has occurred.

How many songs have been written to describe a broken heart? Rock songs. Country songs. Rhythm and Blues. Every music style features a wide selection of songs devoted to heartbreak.

Like this:

"And how can you mend a broken heart?
How can you stop the rain falling down?
Tell me how can you stop the sun from shining?
What makes the world go 'round?"[22]

Whether in song or in conversation, it is commonplace to use words like "heartbroken" and "heartache" to describe a feeling of loss or desperation.

"How can you mend this broken man?
How can a loser ever win?
Somebody please help me mend my broken heart
And let me live again."

This kind of "broken heart" is devastating. In fact, numerous studies have shown that the emotions that accompany this kind of broken heart—anger, depression, hopelessness—actually cause harm to our physical bodies.

"Study after study has shown that people who feel lonely, depressed, and isolated are many times more likely to get sick and die prematurely—not only of heart disease but from virtually all causes—than those who have a sense of connection, love and community."[23]

It is a terrible irony that a broken heart isn't the result of heart disease; it actually *causes* heart disease.

---

[22] Lyrics taken from the song "How Can You Mend a Broken Heart?" by Barry & Robin Gibb. Produced by Robert Stigwood. From the LP *Trafalgar* (Polydor Records, 1971). It was the Bee Gees first U.S. No. 1 single.
[23] Dr. Dean Ornish quoted in the *Los Angeles Times*, "Dr. Dean Ornish on the power of mindful choices." http://articles.latimes.com/2013/feb/23/health/la-he-five-questions-ornish-20130223.

"It turns out that extreme emotions...can have an impact on the electrical impulses of the heart. Studies show that the stress spanning extreme happiness to acute grief has the ability to spur a heart attack. This is due to the body's involuntary and sudden increase in heart rate and blood pressure brought on by a surprising event."[24]

So, why would God require a *broken* heart to change your story?

Because, in God's eyes, a broken heart isn't a heart that has been damaged by loss. It is a heart that is humble before God. It is a heart that sees the good in others and surrenders to the will of God.

So, yes, as strange as it may sound, for your heart to mend, it must actually be "broken."

---

[24] "4 Surprising Heart Attack Triggers." *Cleveland Clinic Health Essentials.* https://health.clevelandclinic.org/2014/01/surprising-heart-attack-triggers/.

# CHAPTER 26

# THE RESPONSE OF A BROKEN HEART

"For this is what the high and exalted One says—He who lives
forever, whose name is holy: 'I live in a high and holy place,
but also with the one who is contrite and
lowly in spirit....'"

**Isaiah 57:15 (NKJV)**

As we have discovered, David's life is a vivid illustration of immense joy, but also one of indescribable pain.

His was a life full of deep relationships *and* deep disappointments.

The story of David and Bathsheba, as recorded in 2 Samuel 11, is one of those disappointments.

It is a story that illustrates just how vulnerable your heart is. Although we tend to think that our hearts are only vulnerable at the lowest points of our lives, that's not true at all. Every day, every season of life, is a prime opportunity for Satan to attack.

Your heart is *always* vulnerable.

In this particular chapter of David's life, he abuses his position and his power, and sins against God in the most appalling fashion. He does so when he is at the very top of his game. David is the king of Israel. He lives in splendor. He has defeated his enemies. He has a loyal and capable staff. He has just demonstrated great generosity to the son of his very dear friend, Jonathan.[25]

Then he stumbles in a terrible way. He commits adultery. Going from bad to worse, he engages in a conspiracy to commit murder.

For this, there is no explanation; there is no acceptable excuse.

David is *guilty*.

It is difficult to fathom that David could fall into such a pit, but he doesn't even seem to understand what he has done! He doesn't

---

[25] See 2 Samuel 9.

comprehend his guilt. In response, God sends the prophet Nathan to confront David.

He tells David this simple story:

> "There were two men in a certain town, one rich and the other poor. The rich man had a very large number of sheep and cattle, but the poor man had nothing except one little ewe lamb he had bought. He raised it, and it grew up with him and his children. It shared his food, drank from his cup and even slept in his arms. It was like a daughter to him.
>
> Now a traveler came to the rich man, but the rich man refrained from taking one of his own sheep or cattle to prepare a meal for the traveler who had come to him. Instead, he took the ewe lamb that belonged to the poor man and prepared it for the one who had come to him."

**2 Samuel 12:1-4**

David responds in an outburst of anger. How could anyone do such a thing? That man is a scoundrel of the *worst* kind. Not only should he pay back what he stole four times over, he should die for such a thing!

Finally, Nathan springs the trap. YOU are that man, he tells David. This is what YOU have done.

With judgment already pronounced, what is David to say? Will he defend himself? Will he blame someone else, or make accusations? What might you have done in similar circumstances when confronted with your mistakes?

> "Then David said to Nathan, 'I have sinned against the Lord.'"

**2 Samuel 12:13**

No blame. No excuses.

The realization of his actions piercing his heart, David immediately humbles himself before God and accepts responsibility. As he reflects on his mistake, he later comes to a very important conclusion, as recorded in the Psalms:

> "The sacrifices of God are a broken spirit, a broken and a contrite heart—these, O God, you will not despise."

### Psalm 51:17 (NKJV)

Now we know why God looked into David's heart and found it to be like His own. Once David was confronted with his sin, his willingness to accept responsibility for his actions and to humble himself before God show the true condition of his heart. His heart was truly "broken."

Is yours?

# CHAPTER 27

# THE HIDDEN PRICE

"If my people, who are called by my name, will humble themselves
and pray and seek my face and turn from their wicked ways,
then I will hear from heaven, and I will forgive their sin
and will heal their land."

**2 Chronicles 7:14**

**D**avid paid a huge price for his sin, both physically *and* emotionally.[26]

We always do.

In fact, it may be that you are struggling through some of those
consequences right now. Is the weight of the past pressing down on
you?

This can be a very big problem on its own, even beyond the actual circumstances of your life. You see, sometimes, just thinking about
how badly you've failed or how far you've fallen prevents you from
changing your story. Your failures get wound up in your mind, and
just *thinking* about the past leaves you hopeless.

It happens when you start thinking these kinds of thoughts:

*"I'm not good enough."*

*"My mistakes are too big."*

*"People won't accept me."*

*"No one could love me."*

What you may fail to see is that you are not alone. On some level,
all of us have been there at some point in our lives. We've questioned
our worth or our abilities. We've even questioned our purpose in life.

This is the power of David's story. In David, we can easily see
ourselves and our own struggles. We can relate to a guy who has

---

[26] See 2 Samuel 12:15-20.

failed like he did. Most importantly, we can see that even the most severe consequences can be overcome.

David lost his son due to his own sin. There may not be anything in life to compare to the weight of guilt that would carry. To know that your actions caused someone you love to suffer or die can be emotionally devastating. For David, the grief during this time of loss was immense.

> "David begged God to spare the child. He went without food and lay all night on the bare ground. The elders of his household pleaded with him to get up and eat with them, but he refused."

**2 Samuel 12:16-17 (NLT)**

David was crushed.

He could easily have given up. He could have completely lost himself and turned away from God. Satan would've claimed yet another victim.

Instead, David found *refuge* in God instead of blame.

> "Have mercy on me, my God, have mercy on me, for in you I take refuge. I will take refuge in the shadow of your wings until the disaster has passed."

**Psalm 57:1**

The apostle Paul, the man formerly known as Saul, the persecutor of Christians, had the same problem. He had been one of the religious elite, a leader, and a man held in high esteem by his peers, right up until he realized the immensity of his sin against God.[27] When God confronted him on the road to Damascus, Paul came face-to-face with the reality of causing the death of innocent people.

Like David, Paul recognized the depth of God's mercy. Here is how he described himself to a young preacher named Timothy:

> "This is a trustworthy saying, and everyone should accept it: "Christ Jesus came into the world to save sinners"— and **I am the worst of them all**. But God had mercy on

---

[27] See Acts 22:1-5 and Philippians 3:4-6.

me so that Christ Jesus could use me as a prime example of his great patience **with even the worst sinners**."

**1 Timothy 1:15-16 (NLT)**

"The *worst* of sinners" was how Paul saw *himself*. Despite this, God rescued him, and called him to a very specific purpose, to preach the very gospel he had denied:

> "Although **I am less than the least** of all the Lord's people, this grace was given me: to preach to the Gentiles the boundless riches of Christ."

**Ephesians 3:8**

Two men of great passion, talent, and promise were confronted by God to account for grievous mistakes. Both men paid a price for those mistakes.

However, both men were also changed. They repented. They demonstrated a truly "broken" heart, a heart deeply grieved by their own actions.

Despite their great failures, they did *not* throw in the towel. Despite the enormity of their mistakes, they did not quit the battle. No, they never denied their weaknesses and their mistakes; instead, they used those mistakes to strengthen their hearts and grow closer to God.

But what about you? No, you may not have murdered Christians, but perhaps your mistakes and your failures may have left you feeling just as guilty. Just as ashamed as David or Paul.

That's exactly what Hayley's story sounds like. After years of heartache and failure and sin, she couldn't see how anyone could possibly value her:

> *I look back on the things I've done and I am disgusted by myself—and I think, how?? How could the CREATOR of everything love me? I didn't even love myself! How could anyone else?*
>
> *Why would He want anything to do with me? How could He have any use for me at all?? How could the Creator of the universe love me? I would've bet that He didn't even like me.*

*BUT GOD—He did, and He does.*

*He loves me and He called me back to Him.*

*It was the most difficult couple of months, filled with lonely nights and brutally honest conversations with God, myself, and with both old and new friends....*

*This life is not easy and being a Christian does not make it all rainbows and butterflies. It's hard and it's messy and it's ugly. But He is so much better and so much more.*

*You look at where I've been, I can sin with the best of them. Hayley the drunk, the gossip, the druggie, the worshipper of false gods, the slut, the hypocrite...you name it, chances are it's been thrown at me and it has fit. I'm really, really messy.*

*You can call me any one of those things...but because of the blood of Christ, He looks past those labels and He calls me chosen, forgiven, daughter, beloved, worthy, adored, HIS.*

**Excerpt from Hayley's Story**

Quite often, the hardest part of allowing God to mend your heart and change your story is that first step of forgiving yourself.

*You must forgive yourself.*

If you don't, you will pay a much more significant price. You will exponentially compound your sense of your mistakes by allowing Satan to convince you that your past mistakes are just too big to fix.

That is nonsense. You are worth saving.

God thinks so, and so should you.

# HEARTWORK EXERCISE NO. 10

$H$umility is often misunderstood. We often believe that word to mean a person that doesn't brag about accomplishments, or isn't arrogant, or doesn't see himself or herself as better than others.

That's not quite right. It's part of the puzzle, but it misses something important.

In his letter to the church at Philippi, Paul explains the idea of humility—as God sees it—very eloquently:

> "Do nothing out of selfish ambition or vain conceit,
> but in humility consider others better than yourselves.
> Each of you should look not only to your own interests, **but also to the interests of others**."

**Philippians 2:3-4**

Quite simply, the humble heart considers the interests of others before it acts.

How often do we act *first*, and consider others later, or not at all?

Understanding humility comes after the realization that we have hurt someone else by acting without regard to their interests. That was David's sin: acting in his own selfish interests without consideration of the other people involved. Once he came to a realization of his sin, he was devastated.

Are there things you have done selfishly, without considering others, that have caused damage to them? Write those things down below. Then, humbly ask God to forgive you. Ask God to bless you with a broken and contrite heart.

# CHAPTER 28

# YOU REAP WHAT YOU SOW

"A wicked person earns deceptive wages, but the one who
sows righteousness reaps a sure reward."

**Proverbs 11:18**

$\mathbf{T}$he Scripture says that a man reaps what he sows.[28]

In regular conversation, people usually say it this way:

*"You got what you deserved."*

*"You asked for it."*

*"You got what was coming to you."*

*"You made your bed; now, you get to lie in it."*

*"You dug your own grave."*

*"You shot yourself in the foot."*

*"What goes around, comes around."*

*"It's nobody's fault but your own."*

As you consider your own life, you may be nodding in agreement.

*"No doubt. That sounds like me. I sure have messed up my life."*

There is some truth in that. When it's all said and done, we are
usually in the circumstances we are in because of *our own* decisions
and *our own* actions. We have typically arrived at our current destination due in part to the many choices *we* have made along the way.

Of course, we can see that with *other* people. The problem is that
we usually struggle to see it within ourselves. Instead, we can describe—in graphic detail—the bad breaks, the bad bounces, and the
bad karma that created our current circumstances.

There is just one problem: we don't see our role in getting there.

---

[28] We previously discussed this in chapter 3.  See Galatians 6:7.

Sure, there are times when we get that life doesn't seem fair, but for the most part, isn't it clear that we are where we are because of the choices we've made?

Perhaps you've not come to that realization yet. Perhaps you insist that it's not your fault at all. Are you telling yourself the truth? Or does your story sound a little like the one below? [You can read this and other real-life stories at www.heartworkministry.com.]

> *At 23, I would say for certain I was a functioning alcoholic, abusing illegal drugs, and using people to my benefit. I was at the bar seven nights a week. I worked hard all day, but when it came time, I was at the bar. That's where all my friends were, or so I thought. I knew I had issues, but I really didn't care what anyone else thought. For the most part, I kept it hidden from those close to me. I was a good liar!*

### Excerpt from Tony's Story

What do you think Tony would say about his choices, of circumstances or of influences?

Do you think they helped him or hurt him?

Tony spent a good part of his life choosing alcohol and drugs, the wrong people, and the wrong places. By his own admission, he was living a lie. Can you see the trap?

Satan seduces you into believing that bad choices are actually good ones. Then, he convinces you to keep it all hidden from everyone else, so that you don't have to confront the truth. Eventually, those bad choices catch up with you. Who do you blame?

Yourself?

Your own poor choices?

No. In an ironic twist, we usually don't even blame the one whose lies we have believed. Instead of recognizing that Satan has held us captive, we turn and ask God why He would allow these things to happen to us!

That is what happened to Tony until he allowed God to mend his heart and change his story.

*I have found peace in this cruel world that will never leave me, simply because of [Celebrate Recovery] and Cedar Point! Cedar Point is a life-changing ministry. I'm living proof of that every day!*

*It takes courage to walk through that door. I respect every one of you for coming in. We're all together in this; we are not ALONE! We can become sober; we can overcome our hurts and habits with Jesus Christ and each other! We have to share our stories; we have to give to others. We need each other; small group is extremely important. It allows us to share more detail of our struggle and how things are each week. It allows me to hear your story and help me. Together we can restore one another.*

How do you find your way out of your current circumstances?

By changing your direction.

By changing your influences.

By surrounding yourself with encouragement and support.

Yes, indeed. You reap what you sow.

# CHAPTER 29

## FINDING SOMEONE TO BLAME

"Don't excuse yourself by saying, 'Look, we didn't know.' For God understands all hearts, and he sees you. He who guards your soul knows you knew. He will repay all people as their actions deserve."

**Proverbs 24:12 (NLT)**

The idea of blaming something or someone else for our problems is something that goes way, way back, all the way back to the begining: as in, the book of Genesis, the book of beginnings.[29]

Think back to our discussion of the story of Adam and Eve in chapter 16. Do you remember the decisions they made? Do you remember the consequences those decisions created for them?

Their failure to obey God is quite surprising when you realize that the only *Do Not* command that existed in the Garden of Eden was **do not** "eat from the tree of the knowledge of good and evil, for when you eat from it you will certainly die."[30]

Satan found a way to make that one "rule" sound oppressive and burdensome. He found a way to make disobedience sound enticing.

> "'You will not certainly die,' the serpent said to the woman. 'For God knows that when you eat from it your eyes will be opened, and you will be like God, knowing good and evil.'
>
> When the woman saw that the fruit of the tree was good for food and pleasing to the eye, and also desirable for gaining wisdom, she took some and ate it."

**Genesis 3:4-6**

Do you see what happened? Satan took the only command God had given to Adam and Eve and managed to convince them that God

---

[29] The word "genesis" means "beginnings."
[30] See Genesis 2:17.

was actually hiding something. He convinced them that God was trying to keep them from *really* living.

Does that sound familiar at all? For example, how many times have you said, or heard someone say, "God would want me to be happy"? That one phrase is used over and over again to justify choices that run completely contrary to what God wants us to do! Sadly, it happens all the time. It's a choice that we make far too often: me rather than God.

When things go badly, do we take responsibility for that choice? Do we recognize the folly of our thoughts?

Look at Adam's response when the Lord confronted his disobedience.

> "The man said, 'The woman you put here with me—
> she gave me some fruit from the tree, and I ate it.'"

**Genesis 3:12**

That sure didn't take long, did it? We're all of three chapters into the Bible, with only two people in the picture, and the blame game has already begun! God says "don't." They "do" anyway. What happens?

*"Not my fault."*

Oh, no, Adam says. It wasn't me. It was *that woman*. This is pretty good evidence that blaming others is a part of our nature; there certainly doesn't appear to be any indication that Adam *learned* to blame others. Can you imagine the alternative? "Yes, God, I disobeyed. My bad. Nobody to blame but me." How often does that happen?

So, if it's our nature to blame someone else for our actions, it means that it takes a conscious decision to take responsibility for our own actions. In other words, blaming others is something that, unless we consciously choose otherwise, we will usually do when confronted with an accusation.

Is the woman in the story any different? Let's examine her response to God.

> "Then the Lord God said to the woman, 'What is this
> you have done?'"

The woman said, "The serpent deceived me, and I ate."

**Genesis 3:13**

Are you detecting a pattern?

Human nature, from the very beginning, has always been to blame something or someone else. This is what Satan does: he convinces you to do something you shouldn't do. How? By convincing you that *you* know better. You know better than your parents. Or God. Or whomever is warning you not to go down a certain path.

*"You will not certainly die...."*

So, people choose poorly, and then blame something or someone else.

How about you? Are you blaming something or someone else?

# CHAPTER 30

# THE THINGS WE DELIGHT IN

"Take delight in the Lord, and he will give you
your heart's desires."

**Psalm 37:4 (NLT)**

**W**hat do you find to be delightful?

In whom do you find delight?

Asked differently, who or what delights you?

It's an important question because the people or the things that you "delight in" will determine the direction of your life. In fact, a man once said that he could tell you everything you needed to know about a man just by looking at his checkbook (back when people actually used checkbooks!).

He wasn't being judgmental. He wasn't playing the 'holier-than-thou' card. He was actually making a very astute observation. His point was that the things on which someone spends his or her money tends to provide a very good idea of what is important to them.

According to Scripture, he is exactly right.

"Wherever your treasure is, there the desires of your
heart will also be."

**Matthew 6:21 (NLT)**

Simply put, the things you get out of life (your treasures) are a direct result of where you put your time and effort (the desires of your heart). Today, we might say it this way: "You get what you pay for."

When things have taken a wrong turn, when you feel lost or adrift in a life seemingly without meaning or purpose, it is usually the result of many small decisions that have piled up into an emotional traffic jam. Suddenly, there seems to be no place to turn. In bitterness, anger, and hopelessness, we blame someone or something else.

In some situations, life simply gets off to a very bad start, and you may have had no control over those circumstances whatsoever. Things like alcoholic parents, physical abuse, or emotional rejection aren't choices anyone would make for himself or herself.

You may feel like you've already been through hell and back, and no one can understand the depth of your pain.

Perhaps you can relate to Tony's tragic story:

> *On June 22nd…my world hit rock bottom. I mean as low as it can get. I only thought I had issues. I had no idea how bad it could get. It was a Saturday and the kids were all at the lake enjoying a day with the boys and their friends….*
>
> *I received a call at 2:00 while at home alone. My grandson, Eric, had been struck by a car and killed instantly. I hit rock bottom. There are no words to describe my pain at that time. It is not humanly possible….*
>
> *I was in shock for several weeks, extremely mad at God, binge drinking, and was headed for a major crash mentally.*

Right in the middle of all that pain and suffering, God put a man in Tony's path that changed his life.

> *I met Tracy that day. Tracy was kind enough to speak that day for our family and our baby boy! I immediately was grateful for him and how he worked so selflessly to get us through that day. There was no way I could ever repay him for what he did for all of us that day. He held all the tiny little pieces we had together somehow!*

Tony's heart had been battered and bruised, but it was still a heart that could be rescued, despite the tragic start to his life, his poor choices, and his disastrous circumstances.

Tony made a choice to find delight in new things; to change the desires of his heart.

> *It was at Cedar Point I learned to build a relationship with Jesus Christ. Cedar Point taught me how to build that relationship. (Celebrate Recovery) taught me how to build it also. He is with me every breath now; I'm in His arms.*

*Jesus has taken my yoke, my worries, and my problems away from me. No more drinking, and the pills are gone. I do wear a patch, but you cannot abuse those. I have not been sober since I was a kid! Never, until now. I received my [one] year chip in January, and I've never been prouder. I'm in the best place I have ever been: life is very peaceful, and life is stable every day.*

Take a step back. Jesus can and *will* rescue you, but you must NOT give up. No matter where you are, or how much you have endured, God can *always* mend your heart.

Yes, He can. He can change *your* story. He can make *your* life whole and fill it with purpose and meaning.

You need to make the decision to let Jesus, the Master Story-Changer, become your focus.

Your delight.

# HeartWork Exercise No. 11

Life is nothing more than a series of choices. If we understand the "good" that God would have us do, and if our delight is in Him, then those choices will consistently be better for us personally. However, Satan preys on our desires to have what *we* want.

> "...but each person is tempted when they are dragged away by their own evil desire and enticed. Then, after desire has conceived, it gives birth to sin, and sin, when it is full-grown, gives birth to death."

**James 1:14-15**

It is our own evil desires—desires that run completely contrary to what God intends for us—that Satan exploits. Eve saw that the fruit was good for food and pleasing to the eye—except that it wasn't. God had already said not to eat from that one tree.

What are those things in life that create distraction for you? Write down the things you know are not really "good" for you.

# PART III

# HEALING YOUR HEART

"And hope does not disappoint us,
because God has poured out His love into our hearts
by the Holy Spirit, whom he has given us."

**Romans 5:5**

The best and most beautiful things in the world
cannot be seen or even touched—
they must be felt with the heart.

**Helen Keller**

# CHAPTER 31

# WHAT GOD WANTS FOR YOU

> "Take to heart all the words I have solemnly declared to you
> this day, so that you may command your children to obey
> carefully all the words of this law. They are not just
> idle words for you—they are your life."

**Deuteronomy 32: 46-47**

The first step in truly healing your heart is to understand who Jesus is and what *HE* wants for you.

The book of John in the New Testament records this incredibly profound statement from Jesus to His disciples:

> "I have come that they might have life, and have it to
> the full."

**John 10:10**

What an incredible promise! Jesus did not come just to give you a life, He came to give you a life that is *full* and abundant. He didn't come to impose burdensome rules on you. Nor did He come, as some might imagine, to allow you to do whatever you please, without judgment.

He came, lived, died, and was resurrected to provide you with the opportunity to live a life full of purpose and meaning, here and now.

However, what we have discovered is that Satan doesn't want you to live that life. So, he battles for your heart. He disguises destruction behind temporary pleasure, tempting you to follow your own path by making those pleasures look and feel attractive. He does everything possible to get you to believe his lies because his victory lies in separating you from God.

Jesus came to deliver this simple message: *open your eyes.*

> "For this people's heart has become calloused; they
> hardly hear with their ears, and they have closed their
> eyes. Otherwise they might see with their eyes, hear

with their ears, **_understand with their hearts_** and turn, and I would heal them."

**Matthew 13:15**

When you begin to understand who God is, you can truly understand with your heart and turn away from Satan. Then God can deliver you from the pain you've experienced.

In fact, He will provide you with detailed instructions on how to live that life of fullness, how to be *truly* happy.

> "Then you will understand what is right and just and fair—every good path. For wisdom will enter your heart, and knowledge will be pleasant to your soul. Discretion will protect you, and understanding will guard you."
>
> **Proverbs 2:9-11**

Unfortunately, popular wisdom would tell you that only *you* can determine what happiness is for you. The general idea is that happiness is subject to individual whim and mostly achieved by pursuing what you want at any given moment.

Way back in November 1989, the Swedish pop duo Roxette hit No. 1 on the Billboard Top 100 with a song called, "Listen to Your Heart." Since then, the song has been covered by a number of other artists, most recently when it was a part of the popular television show *Glee*.

Here is the song's chorus:

"Listen to your heart, when he's calling for you.

Listen to your heart, there's nothing else you can do.

I don't know where you're going and I don't know why,

But listen to your heart, before you tell him goodbye."[31]

The sentiment of the song expresses the typical way people make decisions about their happiness: by listening to their hearts.

Are you making a decision about someone? Listen to your heart. Are you making a decision about your life? Listen to your heart.

---

[31] Lyrics taken from the song "Listen to Your Heart" by Per Gessle and Mats Persson. Produced by Clarence Öfwerman. From the LP *Look Sharp!* (EMI, 1989).

That's fine, of course, when your heart is full of an understanding of those things that *God* tells you are good. When your heart is full of God's wisdom, when you have hidden enough of God's word in your heart that you can resist Satan, then, and only then, can you safely listen to your heart.

Otherwise, you're simply making choices based on selfishness. And, chances are, that isn't working out very well.

But, if you're listening to God, you will understand with your heart as God intended, and He will heal the pain. He will replace your pain with true happiness. That's exactly why Jesus came to earth.

That's what HE wants for you.

# CHAPTER 32

# FINDING TRUE HAPPINESS

*"But may the righteous be glad and rejoice before God;*
*may they be happy and joyful."*

**Psalm 68:3**

**A**ctually, it's quite true. God DEFINITELY wants you to be happy.

There are two critical questions to consider:

What is happiness exactly?

Who determines what will make you happy?

The challenge you face is that Satan will roll out poor, self-serving choices in front of you like a red carpet and convince you it's OK to "listen to your heart" because, after all, "you deserve to be happy."

This is a lie, but, as usual, it possesses just enough truth to lead you down a very bad path. When you choose temporary pleasure as your "happiness," that lie will come back to haunt you at some point.

In the Bible, the book of Matthew contains a section commonly known as the "Beatitudes." They are eight declarations from Jesus of spiritual blessings, and each of those declarations begins with the words, "Blessed are...."[32]

The late Robert Schuller, a long-time pastor, author, and motivational speaker, called these declarations the "Be Happy Attitudes." That's because in the original language of the Bible (Greek), the word for "blessed" is *makarios*, which actually means "happy."

Does God want you to be happy? YES. *ABSOLUTELY!* He tells us exactly how to be happy. *Really* happy. Not short-term happy.

---

[32] The word "beatitude" comes from the Latin word "beatus." When St. Jerome translated the Bible into Latin, the word for happy in each of these verses in Matthew 5 was "beatus" and the noun for of that word is "beatitudo," which translated into the English form of the word, beatitude. From *The Ladder of the Beatitudes,* by James H. Forest (Orbis Books, 1999).

Not substance abuse happy. Not forget-my-problems-for-awhile happy.

Instead, He tells us how to be "blessed" happy, happy as the result of God's blessings.

Remember Psalm 37:4?

> *"Take delight in the Lord,* and he will give you your heart's desires."

Think about those things that you really enjoy—the things that you "take delight in." Are they things that Satan would have you believe are "good" when God has clearly said they are not?

Yes, God does, indeed, want you to be happy! However, as we have seen, it is completely dependent upon the choices you make about the things you delight in. Who will determine what makes you happy? Is it you, or will you let God determine those things in life that are good?

The journey to healing your heart and changing your story is to allow God to determine what is good in your life, not Satan. As he did with Adam and Eve, Satan will tell you just enough truth to get you to believe a lie.

Instead, if you *understand with your heart* the good that is from God, and you turn to Him, He will heal you.

He will bless you with true happiness.

# CHAPTER 33

# THE RIGHT CHOICE

"Don't let anyone capture you with empty philosophies and
high-sounding nonsense that come from human thinking
and from the spiritual powers of this world,
rather than from Christ."

**Colossians 2:8 (NLT)**

In retrospect, our lives can easily be described as a series of decisions.

Throughout your life, you will make dozens of critical decisions. Sadly, we are often guilty of rushing into those decisions with only one thing in mind: ourselves.

As we have noted, one of the biggest lies that Satan will use against you happens when he whispers this in your ear: *"God wants you to be happy."* Of course, Satan isn't sincere about your happiness. It just sounds good.

Our idea of "happiness" may look good on the outside, but the inside can be a completely different story.

> *"In the fall of 2012, the story for our family didn't look very promising. We were in the process of remodeling a new home, had good jobs, and lots of material things, but that is where the positives stopped. However, anyone around us thought we were happy and successful.*
>
> *Addiction, idolatry, pride, and very worldly goals were poisoning us. It seems unreal today to think back on all the decisions and life changes we made without even spending a split second in prayer about them."*

**Excerpt from Mandy's story**

See how good things looked from the outside? Though Mandy describes "good" things—a new home, good jobs, material things—the reality of her family's life was much different.

It is so important to see that *our* definition of happiness comes directly from *our* desires, not from the good that God has determined for us. Our desires will poison our perspectives and do real damage to our lives. Read on as Mandy's story spirals out of control:

> "And it is impossible to please God without faith. Anyone who want to come to him must believe that God exists and that he rewards those who sincerely seek him."
>
> **Hebrews 11:6**

*In October, [my husband] Jerry dove head first into a life of drug addiction and alcoholism. This led to our family spending the next several months apart [and] opened the door to the darkest period of our marriage.*

*The more time he spent living in the world of addiction, the deeper he became trapped. I spent these months desperately trying to get my husband's attention and to control his actions.*

As life gets ugly, we typically want to hide; either we simply stay away from other people, or we crawl down a very dark hole seeking some kind of relief.

Perhaps you are trying to hide right now. Are you avoiding your friends or family? Are you looking for some way to escape?

Here is how Jerry and Mandy began their journey back to real happiness:

> *When I regularly started attending church at Cedar Point, I began to hear God speaking into my life. Instead of spending day after day trying to manipulate Jerry's behavior, I turned him over to God, finally understanding that only He could save Jerry.*
>
> *I began to spend all that time I had previously wasted on worry in prayer. I was surrounded by people at Cedar Point who were encouraging and supported me. As we began to rebuild our lives together, we knew that a lot of lifestyle changes were going to be necessary.*
>
> *Foremost was making God first, in both our lives and our marriage. In a huge step of faith, Jerry left his job to escape the negative influences there. God met us right where we were and walked with us every single step of the way.*

Do you see the changes in Mandy and Jerry's life?

Different choices. Different influences. Different values.

All three of those things are contained in this one profound statement by Mandy:

> *In a huge step of faith, Jerry left his job to escape the negative influences there.*

He made a different choice, one based on faith.

It is a choice that is destined to change his story.

# HEARTWORK EXERCISE NO. 12

$\mathbf{A}$re there choices you have made in your life that you would reconsider now? Write them below. What did you not know or understand at the time you made those decisions?

How would you describe happiness now as compared to when you made the decisions you wrote down?

What is missing in your life that prevents you from experiencing the happiness that God wants you to experience?

# CHAPTER 34

# START WITH A NEW HEART

> "May he strengthen your hearts so that you will be blameless and holy in the presence of our God and Father when our Lord Jesus comes with all his holy ones."

**1 Thessalonians 3:13**

**D**id you know that God has promised you a new heart?

It's true. Although your heart may be battle-scarred, damaged, or completely broken in two, the good news is that you can trade it in for a new one!

In fact, your heart is what God changes *first* in your life when you turn to Him.

> "And I will give you a *new heart*, and I will put a new spirit in you. I will take out your stony, stubborn heart and give you a tender, responsive heart. And I will put my Spirit in you so that you will follow my decrees and be careful to obey my regulations."

**Ezekiel 36:26-27 (NLT)**

Your first decision in your quest to change your story, then, is to decide on Jesus, to submit your will to His. Once you make that decision, God gives you the most precious gift imaginable, a new heart. He also places His Spirit within you.

That is when the tide of battle begins to turn in your favor.

To be clear, God does not say that you will no longer be subject to Satan's deceit. He does not promise that life will suddenly be without challenges, tough choices, or temptation. He does say, however, that He will continually strengthen your heart as you put your trust in Him.

Take the apostle Paul, for example. He certainly knew what it meant to struggle. Read how he describes his life *after* he became a Christ-follower:

"Five different times the Jews gave me thirty-nine lashes. Three times I was beaten with rods. Once I was stoned. Three times I was shipwrecked. Once I spent a whole night and a day adrift at sea. I have traveled many weary miles. I have faced danger from flooded rivers and from robbers. I have faced danger from my own people, the Jews, as well as from the Gentiles. I have faced danger in the cities, in the deserts, and on the stormy seas. And I have faced danger from men who claim to be Christians, but are not. I have lived with weariness and pain and sleepless nights. Often I have been hungry and thirsty and have gone without food. Often I have shivered with cold, without enough clothing to keep me warm."

### 2 Corinthians 11:24-27 (NLT)

Despite these challenges, Paul's faith was unshakeable. His happiness and contentment were centered on Jesus:

"I have learned the secret of being content in any and every situation, whether well fed or hungry, whether living in plenty or in want. I can do everything through him who gives me strength."

### Philippians 4:12-13

You, too, can do *everything* through Him who strengthens your heart. You can find peace. You can know joy. You can live a life of fullness.

It all starts when you replace that old, damaged heart with a brand new one!

# CHAPTER 35

# THE STUMBLING BLOCK OF PRIDE

"Pride leads to disgrace, but with humility comes wisdom."

**Proverbs 11:2 (NLT)**

**P**ride may very well be the biggest stumbling block to healing your heart.

You might call it arrogance, ego, or selfishness, but you can just as easily call it a hard heart. Pride is simply an unwillingness to acknowledge God; it's when you think that you know better than God.

Satan will use pride against you. He will gladly help you erect a wall between you and God, preventing you from mending your heart and changing your story.

> "In his pride, the wicked does not seek Him; in all his thoughts there is no room for God."

**Psalm 10:4**

The remedy, as we read in Proverbs 11:2, is humility—to make the decision to follow God's direction rather than your own. To set pride (ego, conceit, arrogance, stubbornness, selfishness, or hard heart) aside allows God to give you a new heart.

That's exactly what happened in Danyelle's life. When she reached the very bottom, she put her faith in something greater. Sadly, her son's father was not able to do the same.

> *All my relationships with my family were all but gone. I had no one. There were no options. I believed there had to be something more to this life than I had been getting. I was desperate and wanted everything to change. So I gave it a shot.*
>
> *It's so amazing to me how the Lord works!! It was my Son's father (my abuser) that had mentioned Celebrate Recovery. He had*

*gone before. I wanted to check it out. The whole way there he bashed it and talked about how much he had disliked it. But I couldn't afford not to like it. This was my effort to somehow save my life.*

*We went. I LOVED IT. I prayed that night and asked God to line up my path. To give me signs. To show me the way to go. I was more willing now than I had ever been in my whole life.*

### Excerpt from Danyelle's story

He disliked it. She couldn't afford *not* to like it.

He hated it. She LOVED it.

That's pride and humility talking about the same situation. As you will see, the perspectives are completely different.

*I [Danyelle] began to attend [Celebrate Recovery] regularly. I signed up for the next 12-step group. I started reading the Bible. Working the steps. Taking the suggestions that were being given to me. And building relationships there. I began to see some light.*

*At home things were much different. My son's father began using drugs again. He was fired from his job. The abuse turned from mental to emotional. I don't think he liked the change he was seeing in me. He was becoming more angry by the moment.*

There, in vivid detail, is the difference between pride and humility. As Danyelle humbled herself before God and followed His direction, God strengthened her heart.

*I graduated that 12-step class and now have moved on to become a leader in [Celebrate Recovery]. I strive to give back what was so graciously given to me. I have made friendships that will last for eternity. I have a family again.*

*My son and I have moved into our own place now. We wake daily and give thanks to God for it! We love our home.*

*I could go on and on about how my life has changed since I first walked through the doors at Cedar Point church. I'm a miracle!!! I will forever attest to the love of Christ that was poured out to me through the people serving in that building.*

When pride is out of the way, it may surprise you what God can do in your life.

Is your pride a stumbling block?

# CHAPTER 36

# A PRESCRIPTION FOR LIFE

"Whoever of you loves life and desires to see many good days, keep your tongue from evil and your lips from telling lies. **Turn from evil and do good;** seek peace and pursue it."

**Psalm 34:12-14**

It may be that the only thing standing between our broken, pain-ridden lives and a life of fullness and contentment is our own pride or unwillingness to surrender to the will of God, who loves us unconditionally and only wants good for us.

However, God doesn't force you to surrender.

He simply provides you with a choice. Because He is a loving and gracious God, He allows you to make that decision for yourself.

To make the choice to surrender your heart to God is to make a decision that acknowledges who God is, the creator of the universe.[33] It is a decision that acknowledges your need for God.

It is a decision, ultimately, that signals the condition of your heart. It means you have decided to allow God to determine what is good for your life.

God has told us exactly what is GOOD for us:

> "Be careful then, dear brothers and sisters. Make sure that your own hearts are not evil and unbelieving, turning you away from the living God."
>
> **Hebrews 3:12**

"The Lord has told you what is good, and this is what he requires of you: to do what is right, to love mercy, and to walk humbly with your God."

**Micah 6:8 (NLT)**

Do right.

---

[33] Genesis 1:1 says that, "In the beginning, God *created* the heavens and the earth."

Love mercy.

Walk humbly with God.

Perhaps you're surprised. After all, what God prescribes as being "good" for you are things that appear to have little or nothing to do with what you might consider to be "good." But your Creator says specifically that these are the things that are truly good.

To "do right" is to choose God's way. To "love mercy" is to forgive and have compassion on others rather than demanding payment or a pound of flesh. To "walk humbly with God is to acknowledge God as both Savior *and* Lord and to joyfully give yourself to others in exactly the same way that Jesus did.

As Jesus was winding down His ministry, He met with the apostles to teach them one last, very powerful, lesson. As the men sat eating their evening meal, Jesus stood, wrapped a towel around His waist, and began to wash their feet.

Think dusty roads and dirty sandals, and you'll get the idea.

More importantly, understand that by this point, the apostles knew that Jesus was the son of God and the Savior of the world. How strange that must have been!

> "He came to Simon Peter, who said to him, 'Lord, are you going to wash my feet?'
>
> Jesus replied, 'You do not realize now what I am doing, but later you will understand.'
>
> 'No,' said Peter, 'you shall never wash my feet.'
>
> Jesus answered, 'Unless I wash you, you have no part with me.'"

**John 13:6-8**

Peter, who had already acknowledged Jesus as the Messiah, was having nothing to do with it.[34] How could the son of God possibly wash his dirty feet? How degrading for The Master!

Clearly, Jesus needed to teach the apostles what it means to "walk *humbly*" with God.

[34] See Mark 8:27-30.

"I have set you an example that you should do as I have done for you. Very truly I tell you, no servant is greater than his master, nor is a messenger greater than the one who sent him. Now that you know these things, you will be blessed if you do them."

**John 13:15-17**

Jesus, the Master Story-Changer, was prescribing the most powerful remedy imaginable for slaying your pride and changing your story: no matter your station in life, you should focus on helping others.

It is a prescription that will not only remedy your pain, but it will also hasten the healing process.

# HEARTWORK EXERCISE NO. 13

What are you prideful about in your life? What do you refuse to give up or walk away from, even though it's completely destructive to your story?

Consider those questions, then write down those things in your life that you need to confront because your pride is not allowing you to walk away.

# CHAPTER 37

# THE LANGUAGE OF LOVE

"I pray that your love will overflow more and more, and that you will keep on growing in knowledge and understanding."

**Philippians 1:9 (NLT)**

Paul prayed that the church in Philippi would have a "love" that overflows.

What is love, exactly?

Much like the term "broken heart," the word "love" is a bit misunderstood.

In our culture, love is generally used to refer to a feeling, a sexual encounter, a romance, an attitude of tolerance, or even an intense desire for something ("I would love some ice cream!").

In the language of the New Testament (Greek), there are actually several words commonly translated as "love." Rather than use one single word ("love") to describe very different things, the Greeks used four different words:

>   *Eros*: passion or sexual attraction.

>   *Phileo*: brotherly love; natural affection for a close friend.

>   *Storge*: deep affection, especially between parents and children.

>   *Agape*: unconditional, sacrificial love.

In Greek mythology, Eros was the god of love. His Roman counterpart was Cupid. That should probably ring a bell (hopefully some time prior to February 14, if you care to stay out of trouble with your significant other!).

Of the four Greek words that are translated as "love," only the last three are actually used in the New Testament. Although "love" is one of the most common words used in the New Testament, the Greek word *eros*—the word we would most commonly refer to as love in the English language (physical attraction or romance)—is not used at all!<sup>35</sup>

Instead, the most common word for love in the New Testament is the word "agape."

> In John 3:16, it says that "God so loved the world."

> In 1 John 4:8, it says that "God is love."

> In John 15:12, Jesus said, "Love one another, as I have loved you."

In each of these verses, the word translated as "love" is from the Greek word *agape*. And it is *agape* love that allows us to see and treat others the way God intended.

Thankfully, God provides you with that unconditional love. In fact, He pours it into your heart.

> "And hope does not put us to shame, because God's love has been poured out into our hearts through the Holy Spirit, who has been given to us."

> **Romans 5:5**

The important thing to realize is that what God describes as love in the Scripture, the love that He pours into your heart, is not a romantic feeling. It is a willingness to serve others unconditionally.

Understanding that type of love is critical to mending your heart.

---

[35] In the New International Version of the Bible, the different Greek words are translated into the English word "love" 232 times.

# CHAPTER 38

# WHAT'S LOVE GOT TO DO WITH IT?

"The only thing that counts is faith expressing itself through love."

**Galatians 5:6**

So, that intense feeling that we typically describe as "love" is very powerful.

It can move people to do amazing things, even *crazy* things, but that feeling can be fleeting. It might feel conditional. Think about the love that you've experienced. Have you ever wondered why it seems to fade away or fail in the face of difficulty?

The love that the world describes is just a feeling; one that simply fades away when the new wears off. To some, it's nothing more than a "*second-hand* emotion."

> "Oh, what's love got to do, got to do with it?
> What's love but a second-hand emotion?
> What's love got to do, got to do with it?
> Who needs a heart, when a heart can be broken?"[36]

Do you recognize that old song? Many thousands of songs have been written to describe the emotions of romantic love. Have you ever sat and wondered what true, Godly, unconditional love would actually feel like?

When we think of true, romantic love, our thoughts will often turn to marriage. The most common description of love used in a marriage ceremony is taken directly from Scripture. However, it is a description not of *romantic* (eros) love, but of *sacrificial* (agape) love:

---

[36] Lyrics taken from the song "What's Love Got to Do with It?" performed by Tina Turner. Written by Terry Britten and Graham Lyle. From the album *Private Dancer* (Capitol Records, 1984).

"Love is patient, love is kind. It does not envy, it does not boast, it is not proud. It does not dishonor others, it is not self-seeking, it is not easily angered, it keeps no record of wrongs. Love does not delight in evil but rejoices with the truth. It always protects, always trusts, always hopes, always perseveres."

**1 Corinthians 13:4-7**

That is what true love looks like. Make no mistake, this kind of love *feels* pretty awesome!

Think about what love is NOT: impatient, unkind, angry, boastful. Those, of course, are some of the ways we behave when we feel mistreated or unappreciated, we've had a bad day, or we don't particularly care for someone.

The truth is that we cannot love the way God loves without His Spirit, without Him pouring that love into our hearts. It is the miraculous aspect of our relationship with God that He provides us with the necessary ingredients for abundant life when we make the decision to serve Him.

> "Let no debt remain outstanding, except the continuing debt to love one another."
>
> **Romans 13:8**

When you love as God intends, your heart heals and grows stronger each day. As a result, you enrich the lives of the people around you.

That's what love's "got to do with it."

# CHAPTER 39

# TO KNOW HIM IS TO LOVE HIM

"Dear friends, since God so loved us, we also ought to love one another. No one has ever seen God; but if we love one another, God lives in us and his love is made complete in us."

**1 John 4:11-12**

Clearly, God wants us to know and understand love.

As the Scripture says above, when we love one another He *lives* in us, and our love becomes complete through Him.

However, to love one another requires that we learn to love as God intended for us to love. We learn to see other people *as God sees them* rather than how we might see them.

However, as we have learned, the "love" that describes God is quite different from the "love" we normally talk about. What we think of as love—what we typically understand as a feeling or a sense of romance—is not the same love the Bible describes.

No, God's love is not a feeling; it is an *action*. It is a particular way of treating others, whether it is your husband or wife, family, friend, or stranger. It is unconditional. It is given without pretense or expectation.

It is not based on what someone else does or in response to love given *first*.

"But God showed his great love for us by sending Christ to die for us while we were still sinners."

**Romans 5:8 (NLT)**

"We love each other because He loved us first."

**1 John 4:19 (NLT)**

Giving one's life for another has no equal in terms of love. God doesn't require that we die in order to love as Jesus loved. We just have to be willing to give ourselves in service to others.

So, to help us understand what that kind of love looks like in the real world, Jesus shared this simple story:

> "A Jewish man was traveling from Jerusalem down to Jericho, and he was attacked by bandits. They stripped him of his clothes, beat him up, and left him half dead beside the road.
>
> By chance a **priest** came along. But when he saw the man lying there, he crossed to the other side of the road and passed him by. **A temple assistant** walked over and looked at him lying there, but he also passed by on the other side.
>
> Then a despised **Samaritan** came along, and when he saw the man, he felt compassion for him. Going over to him, the Samaritan soothed his wounds with olive oil and wine and bandaged them. Then he put the man on his own donkey and took him to an inn, where he took care of him. The next day he handed the innkeeper two silver coins, telling him, 'Take care of this man. If his bill runs higher than this, I'll pay you the next time I'm here.'
>
> 'Now which of these three would you say was a neighbor to the man who was attacked by bandits?' Jesus asked.
>
> The man replied, 'The one who showed him mercy.'
>
> Then Jesus said, 'Yes, now go and do the same.'"

**Luke 10:30-37 (NLT)**

The key to this story is found in the people who passed by the man who was attacked by bandits. The priest and Temple assistant were both "religious" men, men that we might naturally assume would be helpful to someone in need. However, they didn't help *because* of their religion. To serve as a priest, or to serve in the Temple as an assistant, required that those men remain "clean" according to Old Testament law, and helping a bleeding, dying man would cause them to be "unclean." They viewed their responsibility to their religious practice as more important than helping a dying man!

The Samaritan, on the other hand, was actually an enemy of the Jews! The animosity between Jews and Samaritans stretched back hundreds of years, and their hatred of each other was fierce. However, upon seeing another human being in distress and in need of help, the Samaritan overlooked their differences and, without expectation of repayment, provided for his needs.

That's what love actually looks like, whether between husband and wife, with family, with friends, with strangers, and even with enemies.

Jesus was trying to help the Jews understand that putting religion in front of caring for others was completely wrong; it was something God never taught. In fact, God has always intended that man's first responsibility was to be concerned for the welfare of others.

In the Old Testament law, God had said: "Do not seek revenge or bear a grudge against anyone among your people, but love your neighbor as yourself."[37]

You've probably heard of the "Golden Rule." In the New Testament, Jesus reminded people that God had always intended for them to live by that same rule.

> "So in everything, do to others what you would have them do to you, *for this sums up the Law and the Prophets.*"

**Matthew 7:12**

> "Love your enemies! Do good to them. Lend to them without expecting to be repaid. Then your reward from heaven will be very great, and you will truly be acting as children of the Most High, for he is kind to those who are unthankful and wicked."
>
> **Luke 6:35 (NLT)**

Unfortunately, in today's world, the second most common definition of "love" (after romance or passion) is the idea of "tolerance," but love isn't just the acceptance or tolerance of all things; rather, it is considering the needs of others and providing help in those times of need.

People may argue over what is right or wrong, but accepting something one person considers right and another considers wrong is not *love*. Nor is it "hate" to consider something that someone does as

---

[37] See Leviticus 19:18.

wrong. However, if I were willing to pass by on the other side of the road when that person with whom I may disagree was in need, then I would NOT be loving as God intended.

This is the lesson of the Good Samaritan: that loving others is not conditional, nor is it optional.

In His ministry, Jesus even raised the bar on this idea. It was not enough, He said, to simply treat others the way you would want to be treated. He said, "A new command I give you: Love one another. *As I have loved you*, so you must love one another."[38]

Here's the best news: God wants you to *experience* that love in all its fullness. He wants you to *feel* that love, to *live* that love, to *understand* that love. In his letter to the church in Ephesus, the apostle Paul said that he constantly prayed for the church that they would be *filled* with God's love:

> "And I pray that you, being rooted and established in love, may have power, together with all the Lord's holy people, to grasp how *wide and long and high and deep is the love of Christ*, and to know this love that surpasses knowledge—that you may be filled to the measure of all the fullness of God."

**Ephesians 3:17-19**

Without question, God's greatest desire is for you to know His love intimately and to understand its power in changing your story.

---

[38] See John 13:34.

# HEARTWORK EXERCISE NO. 14

Loving others is not an obligation. It's not about checking a box to complete a requirement. Instead, it is what the heart is led to do in response to God's love for us. As Scripture says in 1 John 4:19, "We love because he first loved us."

Now you know that God's love (*agape*) is an action, not a feeling. It is the process of valuing others and considering their needs and interests to be as important as your own.

> "This is how we know what love is: Jesus Christ laid down his life for us. And we ought to lay down our lives for our brothers and sisters. If anyone has material possessions and sees a brother or sister in need but has no pity on them, how can the love of God be in that person? Dear children, let us not love with words or speech but with actions and in truth."

**1 John 3:16-18**

As your heart mends, how will your actions towards others change? Write some of those actions down below:

# CHAPTER 40

## RESPONDING TO YOUR FAILURES

*"Blessed are the pure in heart for they will see God."*

**Matthew 5:8**

**G**od knows that we will fail.

What He cares about most is how we *respond* to those failures.

As we discussed in chapter 21, when God looks at you, He looks deep into your heart. He is not swayed by money, power, prestige, or any of the other things that might impress people today. Instead, when He peers into your heart, what He sees is your intent and your motives. Although your actions may appear innocent enough to those around you, God always knows what is really going on inside.

The story of the prodigal son is one of the most moving and powerful stories in all the Bible.[39] It is the story of a young man who decides to do as he pleases and squanders the inheritance his father has provided for him.

> "...Jesus told them this story: 'A man had two sons. The younger son told his father, "I want my share of your estate now before you die." So his father agreed to divide his wealth between his sons.
>
> A few days later this younger son packed all his belongings and moved to a distant land, and there he wasted all his money in wild living. About the time his money ran out, a great famine swept over the land, and he began to starve. He persuaded a local farmer to hire him, and the man sent him into his fields to feed the pigs. The young man became so hungry that even the pods

---

[39] The word "prodigal" means to be wastefully extravagant, especially with money.

he was feeding the pigs looked good to him. But no one gave him anything.'"

**Luke 15:11-16 (NLT)**

Imagine the arrogance of asking your father for something you don't actually deserve. An inheritance is something that typically passes from a father to his children upon the father's death, but this young man decided he didn't want to wait that long!

The younger son demands his inheritance, and, piling insult upon injury, he moves far away from his family. Just when it couldn't possibly get any worse, he throws away his money on temporary pleasures until he wakes up and finds himself completely broke.

It seems easy to see the foolishness of those decisions, doesn't it? Sadly, this is a story that plays out over and over again in people's lives. People make bad choices. They squander opportunity. They often hurt those that love them in the process.

How would the prodigal son respond to his failure?

"When he finally came to his senses, he said to himself, 'At home even the hired servants have food enough to spare, and here I am dying of hunger! I will go home to my father and say, "Father, I have sinned against both heaven and you, and I am no longer worthy of being called your son. Please take me on as a hired servant.'

So he returned home to his father. And while he was still a long way off, his father saw him coming. Filled with love and compassion, he ran to his son, embraced him, and kissed him. His son said to him, 'Father, I have sinned against both heaven and you, and I am no longer worthy of being called your son.'

But his father said to the servants, 'Quick! Bring the finest robe in the house and put it on him. Get a ring for his finger and sandals for his feet. And kill the calf we have been fattening. We must celebrate with a feast, for this son of mine was dead and has now returned to life. He was lost, but now he is found.' So the party began."

**Luke 15:17-24 (NLT)**

The responses of both father and son are difficult to believe.

The young son, who earlier in the story seems arrogant and immature beyond comprehension, not only returns home in shame, but also tells his father that he is "no longer worthy" to be called his son. How incredibly difficult would it be to demonstrate that level of humility?

> "Create in me a pure heart, O God, and renew a steadfast spirit within me. Do not cast me from your presence or take your Holy Spirit from me."
>
> **Psalm 51:10-11**

Additionally, the love of the father is so touching. The Scripture says he saw his son coming from "a long way off." It appears that he never gave up on his son and never stopped looking for him to come back to the family. His love and compassion for his son were so overwhelming that he threw a party for his formerly arrogant, immature, selfish son.

Jesus tells this parable to illustrate to His disciples how God actually sees *us* as His people. He was explaining the unwavering love that God has for us! He knows we will fail. He recognizes that we will act selfishly. Still, He waits patiently, watching for us, ready to embrace us as His children again.

Reflect on your current situation. As you look at yourself, do you struggle to figure out how you got to where you are? As you look at your own story, does it seem almost impossible that you have gotten to this point?

This is a critical moment in your journey. The question is, how will you respond? As you confront your past mistakes, what will you do?

When the prodigal son realized how completely he had failed his father, he didn't run.

Nor did he make excuses.

Or blame others.

And he didn't lash out at him. Instead, he fully confessed his sin and his failures—just like David did when he failed so miserably. And what we learn from these stories is that failure is not fatal!

Don't misunderstand. Even as we fail, we should earnestly strive to keep the commands that God gives to us. This is what He told the nation of Israel as they entered the Promised Land in the Old Testament:

> "But be very careful to keep the commandment and the law that Moses the servant of the Lord gave you: to love the Lord your God, to walk in obedience to him, to keep his commands, to hold fast to him and to **serve him with all your heart** and with all your soul."

> **Joshua 22:5**

Yes, sometimes you will falter.

It is how you respond to that failure that reveals the purity of your heart.

# CHAPTER 41

# WHAT PEOPLE DON'T KNOW

"Do not judge, or you too will be judged."

**Matthew 7:1**

We want you to understand that people will have a variety of reactions as you change your story. Some will wish you well, while others will question your sincerity.

Sadly, some will pre-judge your motives. They will see your actions and decide they know *exactly* what is going on and why you're doing what you're doing.

Sometimes they are right, but many times they are wrong. It's a lesson for all of us to learn; it's never a good idea to be in the business of making the assumption that you know why someone is doing something.

Don't be discouraged! God sees your heart, and He walks right beside you as it is healing.

Again, David's life is an example.

You know the story of David's battle with Goliath, but let's go back and look at the events that led to that epic fight.

> "Now Jesse said to his son David, 'Take this ephah (about a bushel) of roasted grain and these ten loaves of bread for your brothers and hurry to their camp. Take along these ten cheeses to the commander of their unit. See how your brothers are and bring back some assurance from them. They are with Saul and all the men of Israel in the Valley of Elah, fighting against the Philistines.'"

**1 Samuel 17:17-19**

So David does exactly as his father instructed him. He gathers the food, leaves his flock in the care of another shepherd, and travels to where the Israelites are faced off against their enemy, the Philistines. As David runs to the battle line to find his brothers, he hears Goliath challenging the Israelites.

*Mocking* them. *Insulting* them. *Defying* them.

It's more than David can stand.

> "David asked the men standing near him, 'What will be done for the man who kills this Philistine and removes this disgrace from Israel? Who is this uncircumcised Philistine that he should defy the armies of the living God?' When Eliab, David's oldest brother, heard him speaking with the men, he burned with anger at him and asked, 'Why have you come down here? And with whom did you leave those few sheep in the wilderness? *I know how conceited you are and how wicked your heart is; you came down only to watch the battle.*'"

**1 Samuel 17:26-28**

Wow! Notice how Eliab characterizes his younger brother.

He says:

"I *know* how conceited you are…"

"I *know* how wicked your heart is…"

"I *know* why you are here."

Why does David's brother react this way?

> "Stop judging by mere appearances, but instead judge correctly."
>
> **John 7:24**

Is he embarrassed by his brother's impudence? Is his pride hurt that his younger brother would have the courage he cannot find? Does he *really* think David has a wicked heart? Or is it simply the stress and the emotion of the moment that causes him to say something he shouldn't?

The most important question is this: *How is it that God sees David's good heart and David's own brother does not?*

Most importantly, know that it is always a very bad idea to look at someone else and judge their motives.

You are changing *your* story.

They can change their story, too.

# CHAPTER 42

# WHO ARE YOU REALLY?

"The purposes of a person's heart are deep waters, but one who has insight draws them out."

**Proverbs 20:5**

With careful observation, people eventually see you for who you really are.

Those conclusions should *not* be based on how you look, what you have, or where you live. It should be based on your actions: the things you consistently say and do.

Again, the things you *consistently* say and do.

The truth is that a good-hearted person can, and will, make mistakes. As you redirect your life and God changes your story, you won't be perfect. Just as fruit identifies the type of tree, so our *consistent* words and actions identify our hearts.

> "A good man brings good things out of the good stored up in his heart, and an evil man brings evil things out of the evil stored up in his heart. *For the mouth speaks what the heart is full of.*"
>
> **Luke 6:45**

Creating and maintaining a pure heart requires your active participation.

It all begins when God gives you a new start and replaces your damaged heart with a new one (chapter 34). It continues when He pours out His spirit and His love into that heart.[40]

Then, God provides you with the means to protect and nurture your heart.

---

[40] See Romans 5:5.

This is where the Scripture plays such an important role in your journey. It allows you to put the right things into your heart, those things that God has already determined will allow you to lead an abundant life.

> "All Scripture is inspired by God and is useful to teach us what is true and to make us realize what is wrong in our lives. It corrects us when we are wrong and teaches us to do what is right."

**2 Timothy 3:16 (NLT)**

Yes, it may take some time to change your habits. It may take some time to purify the depths of your heart. Remember that God is patient, not willing that anyone should lose hope or fall away.[41]

As you change the things you consistently say and do to be His words and His actions, you will be changing who you really are.

> "Thank you for being a part of showing me the real side of loving God and being a Christian, where I don't feel like I have to live in this plastic bubble, afraid to breathe wrong and in fear of living life. Even after all these years, it is your actions, along with your wise words, and especially your humor, that have continued to have such a positive impact on my life."
>
> **A former member of Cedar Point Church**

---

[41] See 2 Peter 3:9.

# HeartWork Exercise No. 15

**P**aul said, "Don't worry about anything; instead, pray about everything. Tell God what you need, and thank Him for all he has done."[42]

Prayer is a very important aspect of healing your heart and changing your story. Praying to God is just like talking with anyone you care about; it is how you build the relationship and develop trust. The more you can open your heart directly to God, the more He can provide comfort and encouragement.

What are you worrying about? What parts of your life do you need to unload?

Jesus said, "Come to me, all of you who are weary and carry heavy burdens, and I will give you rest."[43] Isn't it reassuring to know that God not only welcomes you, but He also encourages you to dump all the challenges of your life on His shoulders?

Write down the things that you need to give to God in prayer. God already knows, but unloading those burdens will do miracles for your heart.

---

[42] See Philippians 4:6 (NLT).
[43] See Matthew 11:28 (NLT).

# PART IV

# CHANGING YOUR STORY

"Wisdom will save you from the ways of wicked men,
from men whose words are perverse, who have left the
straight paths to walk in dark ways, who delight in doing wrong
and rejoice in the perverseness of evil, whose paths are
crooked and who are devious in their ways."

**Proverbs 2:12-15**

"Prayer is not asking. It is a longing of the soul.
It is daily admission of one's weakness.
It is better in prayer to have a heart without words
than words without a heart."

**Mahatma Gandhi**

# CHAPTER 43

## A BRAND NEW JOURNEY

*"'For I know the plans I have for you,' declares the Lord,*
*'plans to prosper you and not to harm you, plans to*
*give you hope and a future.'"*

**Jeremiah 29:11**

$A$re you convinced that your story doesn't have to end in disappointment or tragedy?

Believe it!

Be encouraged!

This may be the first time you've experienced hope in a very long while.

However, you may have suddenly realized that change can be very difficult. Doing things differently is not always as easy as it may appear. Thinking about a different story is one thing; doing things differently can be quite another.

There is a reason for that. It's because things in motion *tend to stay in motion.*

Sir Isaac Newton is credited with "discovering" this scientific idea in 1687. In fact, it is the first of what is known as Newton's three Laws of Motion, and is often referred to as the *law of inertia*. It says that things at rest tend to stay at rest, and things in motion tend to stay in motion.

This is true in the world of physics. It is usually true in our lives as well.

Literally, it can be very difficult to overcome the *inertia* of our lives. Choosing a different direction in life rarely happens without difficulty. In many cases, it can seem quite impossible. After all, why do people struggle to keep New Year's resolutions? Why do people fail to do things they *know* they should do?

Quite often, it's not that we don't *want* to do those things; it's just that we find it much too easy to continue down the same path.

There is a second part to Newton's law of inertia. Specifically, the law states that objects tend to keep doing what they are currently doing, *unless acted upon by an unbalanced force*. In other words, things tend to keep moving in the same direction unless something acts upon the object with enough force to cause a change.

That is also true in our lives, isn't it? Many times, we want to change, we know we *need* to change, but it will almost never happen until that "unbalanced force" occurs. In our lives, that "unbalanced force" can be an event or a person, but it is always something that simply cannot be ignored. Quite often, it is a blinding revelation (an "Aha!" moment) when we realize that we simply cannot continue on the current path without dire consequences.

However, unlike the object in motion, which has no choice in the matter and simply changes direction due to the external force that is applied, you will have to make a choice. You can choose to give up or you can choose to give in. In either case, you will arrive at a *decision*. When that decision is to change direction—and that decision is made in your heart with absolutely no turning back—then the process of real change can truly start.

In chapter 7, we introduced you to Andrew. His life had spiraled downhill so long and so far that it is difficult to envision how he ever recovered. In his own words, it came down to one defining moment when his heart became convinced that change was no longer an option:

> *"It was one of these times in [the detox unit in jail] that I broke down and asked Jesus into my heart. People throw this phrase around a lot, but it never rang more true than in that moment. I was sick and tired of being sick and tired. I lied (sic) there on my half-inch thick mat, surrounded by cold concrete in a ten-by-eight foot room with however many other people. I pulled my wool/assorted recycled material blanket up over my head and I whispered a drowning man's 'save me' prayer. In that moment I knew in my heart, in the very core of my being, that I never had to feel that way again."*

**Excerpt from Andrew's Story**

Andrew's life had so much momentum in the direction of destruction that the feelings he experienced could have overwhelmed him. For him to change direction required an "unbalanced force" so powerful that the decision could no longer be avoided or postponed.

That event was the gut-wrenching pain of addiction withdrawal.

The physical symptoms associated with withdrawal include muscle cramps, breathing difficulty, nausea, seizures — and worse. For Andrew, enough was finally enough.

Your story will not end in disappointment. Your story will change.

In this new journey, you never have to feel that way again.

# CHAPTER 44

# REBUILDING YOUR WALLS

"Some of you will rebuild the deserted ruins of your cities.
Then you will be known as a rebuilder of walls
and a restorer of homes."

**Isaiah 58:12 (NLT)**

Long, long ago, the walls of an ancient city were critically important to the welfare of that city.

Those walls served as a crucial line of defense against potential enemies. Not only did the walls prevent enemies from easily entering or attacking the city, but the towers and fortifications in the wall also provided 'high ground' that made the city much easier to defend.

If, for some reason, those walls were significantly damaged or destroyed, the city became quite vulnerable to attack.

Stop for a moment. Think of your heart as that ancient city, a city in desperate need of protection from surrounding enemies. Now, think of your life as the walls of that city. If the walls of your life are damaged, your heart is at risk. Rebuilding those walls—changing your story—is critical to protecting your heart.

That is what the book of Nehemiah is all about.

The story of Nehemiah is found in a book of the same name in the Old Testament. The story occurs during a time when God has allowed Israel to be taken captive by an enemy nation. At that time, Nehemiah, a Jew, worked in the service of the king of Persia. As the story unfolds, Nehemiah learns that the walls of his beloved Jerusalem have been torn down and the gates destroyed by fire.

In order to understand the impact this has on Nehemiah, you must understand the importance of the city of Jerusalem. Jerusalem, the city of David, means everything to Nehemiah. His entire identity as a Jew is wrapped up in the city of Jerusalem.

It is not only *his* home; it is home to the throne of his God.

"When I heard this, I sat down and wept. In fact, for days I mourned, fasted, and prayed to the God of heaven. Then I said, 'O Lord, God of heaven, the great and awesome God who keeps his covenant of unfailing love with those who love him and obey his commands, listen to my prayer! Look down and see me praying night and day for your people Israel. I confess that we have sinned against you. Yes, even my own family and I have sinned! We have sinned terribly by not obeying the commands, decrees, and regulations that you gave us through your servant Moses.'"

**Nehemiah 1:4-7**

> "Let us rebuild the wall of Jerusalem and end this disgrace!"
>
> **Nehemiah 2:17**

Overwhelmed by the news, Nehemiah makes a decision. *He* will take on the task of rebuilding the walls of his beloved city. The very thought of his city unprotected and vulnerable is quite enough to jolt him into action. The problem? This is a city that is hundreds of miles away. Also, by the way, Nehemiah is not exactly a construction guy. He is a *cupbearer* to the king.[44]

Nehemiah's first actions may seem a bit odd. He doesn't immediately leave for Jerusalem; instead, he first humbles himself before God. He fasts and prays. Most importantly, Nehemiah confesses sin. He takes responsibility for his own actions, and he acknowledges the sins of Israel.

Notice that he doesn't blame God. He doesn't blame others. He doesn't make excuses. Instead, he says, "We have sinned against you."

Following Nehemiah's example, the first step in changing your story is to approach God humbly and confess your mistakes. No, God doesn't need it, but you do. You need to take responsibility for your own decisions and your own actions. That is not to say that some parts of your circumstances haven't been outside of your control; it is likely that some parts of your journey are a result of your

---

[44] See Nehemiah 1:11.

background or your family or other circumstances. You can't control those things any more than Nehemiah could control the actions of the people of Israel.

What you can control—what you *can* change—is you.

You can get busy rebuilding your walls.

# CHAPTER 45

# THE ROAD BACK

"If at that time you and your children return to the Lord your God, and if you obey with all your heart and all your soul all the commands I have given you today, then the Lord your God will restore your fortunes...."

**Deuteronomy 30:2-3 (NLT)**

Your journey didn't get sidetracked overnight.

No possible way.

In fact, your journey is much like those ancient city walls that have decayed and crumbled through many years of exposure and neglect. It isn't reasonable to assume that you can put all the pieces back together in a short time.

Your walls may have been battered and beaten by the winds of time and the onslaught of enemies, and the physical and emotional impact of those years of bitterness and hurt may be substantial.

You may need to overcome years of bad habits. You have to remedy years of bad choices.

Once the walls of your life have fallen into disrepair, they must be rebuilt, or your heart lies completely exposed to the enemy. That rebuilding process is going to take some time: time to change, time to heal, and time to grow.

In chapter 1, we shared Jena's story. It is a scary example of the damage that can be done to a life over time. Although most stories aren't as dramatic as hers, variations with similar details are far more common than many of us might imagine. Take a moment to read it again (you can read the entire story at www.heartworkministry.com), and notice how her life just spirals out of control:

*My mother passed when I was 12 in a tragic car accident.*

*By the time I was 14, I started drowning my pain in alcohol, and my brother traded his guilt and pain for IV drugs. By the time I was 15, he had entered his first stint in rehab. His drug abuse would continue for the next 20 years.*

*When I was 16, I became a mother to my first child. She was a blessing in disguise. Had God not sent her to me, I am unsure of what path my life would have taken. I knew my only goal was to be the mother to her that I was missing in my life. My father asked me to leave my home with my daughter, so we did. Life only became harder.*

*When I was 18, and living on my own, I gave birth to my second daughter and was married to their father. One night while I was at work, the phone rang. It was my husband informing me that my daughter was not breathing and to come home immediately. When I arrived home it was too late. She was gone. I buried her 10 days later on my 19th birthday.*

*Nine months after, my husband was arrested, and soon after convicted for first degree murder of our child and sentenced to life in prison. Again my world was demolished. My baby was taken away from me and I was married to the man who had taken her away.*

*My reality was shattered. I remember asking God why he would give me this angel only to take her from me so soon and in such a tragic way. My life was in shambles. That was my rock bottom, or so I thought.*

*Little did I know I was pregnant with my 3ʳᵈ child when my (then) husband was sent to prison.*

### Excerpt from Jena's Story

Pain. Alcohol. Drugs. Prison. Death.

Try to imagine the toll on her life. If you've been there—or you're living it out right now—you *can* imagine. Many people, like Jena, get so far off the beaten path that they feel like there is no hope whatsoever. That's Satan working on you again; *any* story can be changed.

Perhaps your life is simply adrift: your marriage is a mess, or life seems to be a struggle, or you are yearning for something more meaningful. Know that God is calling to you just as loudly as He was to Jena.

That is not to claim that it will be easy or that the road back isn't tough.

No, it's not always easy, but it is *always* possible.

When you return, God awaits, ready to restore you to an abundant life.

# HeartWork Exercise No. 16

There are a lot of things to do in order to change your story. It will begin with a change in direction, and, in most cases, you will need to change your current circumstances and/or the influences around you.

Trying to do it alone can be overwhelming. Finding a church home and a group of people who can stand with you is very important. Changing your story starts with that first step—the courage to ask someone for help.

Who is that someone for you? If you don't know anyone, look for Celebrate Recovery® in your area or a church that is reaching out to the community.

Write down some of the possibilities below: Reflect on a church, an outreach, or an individual that you know that can help you through this process.

# CHAPTER 46

## THE COURAGE TO ASK

"But in my distress I cried out to the Lord; yes, I prayed to my God for help. He heard me from his sanctuary; my cry to him reached his ears."

**Psalms 18:6 (NLT)**

Nehemiah's story is a story of leadership in a crisis.

It is also a primer in how to accomplish great things.

Most importantly, it is a lesson in how you can change your story.

In fact, the reason that the story of the rebuilding of the walls of Jerusalem is such an incredible lesson is because it is mirrors life so perfectly.

The challenge that confronts Nehemiah is an intimidating one. After his arrival in Jerusalem, he examines the city walls and then announces to the people that, with God's help, he intends to rebuild the walls and restore the city's former glory. At first, the people are enthusiastic about the project, but the excitement fades quickly as problems arise. First, the enemies of change gossip and make up lies. Then, they begin to actively resist and even try to destroy Nehemiah.[45]

Sounds a bit like life, doesn't it?

There is so much to learn from Nehemiah and the way in which he overcomes the many challenges he encounters. First, he creates a detailed plan, one that requires a great number of people to contribute.[46] *He doesn't just show up with a few tools and get busy.*

Then, he inspires people to help. He assigns groups to each task. Each family in Jerusalem repairs the part of the wall that is in front of their own home. *He doesn't try to do it by himself.*

---

[45] Read the entire story of Nehemiah's leadership in rebuilding the walls of Jerusalem in the Old Testament book of Nehemiah, chapters 2-6.
[46] See Nehemiah 3.

When he encounters resistance, his first step is to ask for God's guidance. *He doesn't try to control things on his own.*

Finally, at every point where he encounters difficulty, he adjusts the plan to counter the enemy. *He refuses to give up.*

What we learn is that rebuilding our walls, like changing our stories, is a process. It is a process that may require you to overcome a lot of challenges. There will almost certainly be resistance. There *will* be struggles.

In fact, Nehemiah encountered adversity from the very beginning:

> "Sanballat was very angry when he learned that we were rebuilding the wall. He flew into a rage and mocked the Jews, saying in front of his friends and the Samarian army officers, 'What does this bunch of poor, feeble Jews think they're doing? Do they think they can build the wall in a single day by just offering a few sacrifices? Do they actually think they can make something of stones from a rubbish heap—and charred ones at that?'
>
> Tobiah the Ammonite, who was standing beside him, remarked, 'That stone wall would collapse if even a fox walked along the top of it!'
>
> Then I prayed, 'Hear us, our God, for we are being mocked.'"

**Nehemiah 4:1-4 (NLT)**

In real life, it is often quite tempting to give up at the first sign of adversity. Change is hard enough without resistance from others. Despite this, Nehemiah's first thought is always to go to God in prayer and ask for help.

As the people continue to labor on the walls and reach the halfway point, the enemy continues to harass them at every turn.

> "But when Sanballat and Tobiah and the Arabs, Ammonites, and Ashdodites heard that the work was going ahead and that the gaps in the wall of Jerusalem were being repaired, they were furious. They all made

plans to come and fight against Jerusalem and throw us into confusion."

**Nehemiah 4:7-8 (NLT)**

Now, the resistance is progressing beyond mere words. The enemy has taken to actively fighting against Nehemiah.

Everyone who has ever struggled to change his or her story will describe something very similar. Quite often, there are people who don't want your story to change, and Satan will use them in every way possible to discourage you.

Sometimes the resistance just seems overwhelming.

> "Then the people of Judah began to complain, 'The workers are getting tired, and there is so much rubble to be moved. We will never be able to build the wall by ourselves.'
>
> Meanwhile, our enemies were saying, 'Before they know what's happening, we will swoop down on them and kill them and end their work.'
>
> The Jews who lived near the enemy came and told us again and again, 'They will come from all directions and attack us!'"

**Nehemiah 4:10-12 (NLT)**

For Nehemiah, this was absolutely the most critical stage of rebuilding the walls of Jerusalem. It would have been easy, maybe even understandable, for Nehemiah to call it quits. Everyone and everything just seemed to be against him.

That time may come in your journey. It will be the most critical time in the process of changing your story. You will want to change. You will know you need to change. You won't be able to imagine going back to a life of pain, bitterness, and anger.

*What will you do?*

Here is what Nehemiah did: He prayed diligently for God's help. He made more adjustments. He never quit encouraging the people.

He never quit giving them heart.

"So I placed armed guards behind the lowest parts of the wall in the exposed areas. I stationed the people to stand guard by families, armed with swords, spears, and bows.

Then as I looked over the situation, I called together the nobles and the rest of the people and said to them, 'Don't be afraid of the enemy! **Remember the Lord, who is great and glorious, and fight** for your brothers, your sons, your daughters, your wives, and your homes!'

When our enemies heard that we knew of their plans and that God had frustrated them, we all returned to our work on the wall. But from then on, only half my men worked while the other half stood guard with spears, shields, bows, and coats of mail. The leaders stationed themselves behind the people of Judah who were building the wall. The laborers carried on their work with one hand supporting their load and one hand holding a weapon. All the builders had a sword belted to their side. The trumpeter stayed with me to sound the alarm.

Then I explained to the nobles and officials and all the people, 'The work is very spread out, and we are widely separated from each other along the wall. When you hear the blast of the trumpet, rush to wherever it is sounding. **Then our God will fight for us!**'"

**Nehemiah 4:13-20 (NLT)**

You are going to need help, too. You are going to need encouragement. There will probably be times when you need to "sound the trumpet" and call for help.

It is critically important to know that there are people around you who understand your struggles and are willing to help. In fact, just knowing that people stand at the ready—that they have stationed themselves around you and are prepared to fight with you—will often be the encouragement you need to change your story.

That certainly was the case for Jena:

*A friend from work had introduced me to Cedar Point Church and I attended weekly.*

*It always felt as though Pastor Rick was speaking directly to me in his sermons. I would sit in the back so that no one would see me cry, and I could remain invisible. I was looking to my Heavenly Father to comfort me and give me direction but did not know how or if he would hear my prayers. Each week I would add my brother to the prayer list in church, hoping somehow it would help him.*

*One day, I built up the courage to give Pastor my phone number and asked him to call me, which he did. I remember pouring my heart out on that phone call, uncertain of how he would react, and hoping I would not be judged. Pastor stopped me and said, "Jena, let's pray." And we did. I was never judged; only loved.*

*That was the beginning of my new relationship with my Lord and Savior and the beginning of my new forever family. I had never felt so lost and alone yet Cedar Point made me realize they are there to see me through all of my pain. They helped me see that God has incredible things in store for me and my family. I was soon baptized at the church picnic. I couldn't hold back my tears of indescribable joy. All of my past suddenly became just that; my past. My journey through this painful life led me to this point and to this place and I can never express how my heart and soul have forever changed.*

**Excerpt from Jena's story**

It took a while, but Jena finally sounded the trumpet.

When she did, *they* were there. *They* helped her, which was exactly what Jena needed as she worked to rebuild her walls.

When the time comes, will you find the courage to ask God for help?

He *will* answer.

# CHAPTER 47

# THE MOST IMPORTANT THING

"For what I received I passed on to you as of first importance: that Christ died for our sins according to the Scriptures, that he was buried, that he was raised on the third day according to the Scriptures...."

**1 Corinthians 15:3-4**

C.S. Lewis is one of the foremost Christian thinkers of our time.

We're sure you've heard of him, or at least you've heard of some of his writings. Among other classic works, he wrote *Chronicles of Narnia* and *The Screwtape Letters*.[47]

Coincidentally, he was also a close friend of J. R. R. Tolkien, the writer who created the classic stories, *The Hobbit* and *The Lord of the Rings*.

Lewis was also an atheist. Although he had been raised in a religious family, by the age of 15 he had already moved away from Christianity. It wasn't until the age of 32 that he turned back to Christianity, due in no small part to his many discussions with Tolkien.

During World War II, Lewis spoke regularly on the religious programming of the British Broadcasting Corporation (BBC). Eventually, transcripts of those broadcasts were published in a compelling book called *Mere Christianity*.

It was about this same time that Lewis also wrote an essay entitled *First and Second Things*, in which he spoke of the priorities of life:

> "When I have learnt to love God better than my earthly dearest, I shall love my earthly dearest better than I do now. Insofar as I learn to love my earthly dearest at the expense of God and instead of God, I

---

[47] Film adaptations have been made of three of the seven books included in *The Chronicles of Narnia*, including *The Lion, the Witch, and the Wardrobe* (Walt Disney Pictures and Walden Media, 2005), *Prince Caspian* (Walt Disney Pictures and Walden Media, 2008) and *The Voyage of the Dawn Treader* (Fox 2000 Pictures and Walden Media, 2010).

shall be moving towards the state in which I shall not love my earthly dearest at all.

When first things are put first, second things are not suppressed but increased."

Lewis believed that loving God *first* would necessarily lead a person to love family as well. He considered how focusing on family first at the expense of God might easily lead one to neglect love for his family. He believed that loving one's family while neglecting the very source of that love (God) could put the love for family at risk.

In a letter written in 1951, Lewis clarified his thinking with these words:

"Put first things first, and we get second things thrown in; put second things first, and we lose both first and second things."

This sentiment—putting the most important things first—is critically important in your journey. Changing your story is fully dependent upon your decision to put the most important thing first, prioritizing the commitment of your heart to change direction.

Going to church, finding some Christian friends, and giving up one of your vices are all good things, but ultimately they are "second" things. These efforts can easily fail if your heart is not fully given to changing direction and fully humbled before God. Your "first" thing, the most important thing, is to develop a heart that is unwilling to compromise, unwilling to walk close to the line of your former life.

In practical terms, it sounds like the proclamation made by Joshua once the Israelites had fled Egypt and moved into the land promised to Abraham:

"But if serving the Lord seems undesirable to you, then choose for yourselves this day whom you will serve, whether the gods your ancestors served beyond the Euphrates, or the gods of the Amorites, in whose land you are living. *But as for me and my household, we will serve the Lord.*"

**Joshua 24:15**

In the New Testament, the book of James says it this way: "Anyone who chooses to be a friend of the world becomes an enemy of God."[48] The implication is very clear—there is no middle ground.

Changing direction means making Jesus the Lord of your life. Everything else will follow once you've completely committed yourself to that decision.

That is the most important thing.

---

[48] See James 4:4.

# CHAPTER 48

# THE STRENGTH TO ENDURE

"He gives strength to the weary and increases the
power of the weak."

**Isaiah 40:29**

**H**ow long do you think the average New Year's resolution lasts?

It is at the beginning of a New Year that many people decide they need to change something. Actually, in most cases, what people decide to do is make a resolution; they may want to change, but making a resolution is not always the same as making a change. We know that's true because most people who make resolutions don't change at all.

According to research, these are the most common changes that people resolve to make:

1. Lose weight
2. Get organized
3. Spend less and save more
4. Enjoy life to the fullest
5. Stay fit and healthy
6. Learn something exciting
7. Quit smoking[49]

Not surprisingly, according to the *Journal of Clinical Psychology*, one out of every four people has already given up on their resolution by the end of the first week in January! By January 31, only two out of every three people are still holding on to their resolutions.

How many people actually follow all the way through? How many people not only resolve to change, but actually change? According to research, for every twelve people who set a New Year's resolution,

---

[49] Retrieved from http://www.statisticbrain.com/new-years-resolution-statistics/.

only about one person—on average, only 8 percent of people—will actually follow through to the end.

The reason is pretty simple. It's that third law of motion. To make any of those life changes listed above requires a complete change of direction, and people don't think about how difficult it is to change momentum. They believe that the resolution will somehow magically make the change a reality!

> "It is God who arms me with strength and keeps my way secure."
>
> **2 Samuel 22:33**

Without a change of heart—a clear decision to do things differently—the mind will too easily give up to its resistance to change.

Remember this: the mind can decide, but until the heart has moved "all-in" on the idea, it is difficult for the mind to create the plans to make changing direction possible. As we like to say, the mind can be convinced, but until the heart is convicted nothing will really change.

We don't want you to be blindsided. Once you make that critical decision to change directions, you know that you will likely run into all manner of resistance. This is exactly why New Year's resolutions rarely succeed. If there were never any resistance involved, losing weight or quitting smoking would be much easier!

Do you remember the Old Testament story of Moses and Pharaoh? (Maybe you saw the classic movie *The Ten Commandments* with Charlton Heston.[50]) It is the Bible story of how God rescued the Israelites from slavery in Egypt. He called Moses, a man who had been born an Israelite but raised as an Egyptian, to convince Pharaoh to allow the Israelite people to leave Egypt. The problem is that Pharaoh didn't have any interest in letting the Israelites leave. After all, they were slaves, a huge source of free labor that Pharaoh was exploiting for his own purposes.

God, through a series of miracles delivered by Moses, persuaded Pharaoh to change his mind, and Pharaoh finally surrendered and

---

[50] *The Ten Commandments*. Paramount Pictures (1956). Directed and produced by Cecil B. Demille.

allowed Moses to lead the people out of Egypt. However, upon leaving Egypt, God doesn't lead the Israelites on the most direct route to their destination. Why? God knows that mankind is often quite lacking in the courage necessary to change.

> "When Pharaoh let the people go, God did not lead them on the road through the Philistine country, though that was shorter. For God said, 'If they face war, they might change their minds and return to Egypt.'"

**Exodus 13:17**

Even though the Israelites were in bondage and begged for deliverance, God knew they could easily change their minds: not because they wanted to be slaves, but because the prospect of fighting the Philistines would be even worse in their minds. Yes, sometimes, people prefer slavery to freedom when that freedom requires the possibility of sacrifice.

So it is in our lives. Sometimes, significant resistance to change will cause you to want to give up. That resistance can arrive in many forms: discouragement, criticism, temptation, conflict, and many other things. You may find that it is easier to give in than to persevere.

That is, unless your heart is fully convicted, and you have placed your faith in changing your story in the hands of the Master Story-Changer.

> "No temptation has overtaken you except what is common to mankind. And God is faithful; he will not let you be tempted beyond what you can bear. But when you are tempted, he will also provide a way out **so that you can endure it.**"
>
> **1 Corinthians 10:13**

# HeartWork Exercise No. 17

In the Old Testament, Solomon followed in his father David's footsteps and became king over Israel. During his reign, he labored for seven years to build a temple in which the people would worship God.

As Solomon dedicated the temple, he prayed fervently that God might give his people a second chance if they were ever to fall away from God. It is an interesting prayer because Solomon seems to know that people are inherently given to poor decisions, or maybe he just understood his own weaknesses.

Solomon also realized that people are capable of change, even when they wind up down the wrong path. Here is part of his dedication prayer:

> "When they sin against you—for there is no one who does not sin—and you become angry with them and give them over to their enemies, who take them captive to their own lands, far away or near; and if they have a change of heart in the land where they are held captive, and repent and plead with you in the land of their captors and say, 'We have sinned, we have done wrong, we have acted wickedly'; and **if they turn back to you with all their heart and soul** in the land of their enemies who took them captive, and pray to you toward the land you gave their ancestors, toward the city you have chosen and the temple I have built for your Name; then from heaven, your dwelling place, hear their prayer and their plea, and uphold their cause."

**1 Kings 8:46-49**

Solomon realized that the heart of man was the key.

Where is your heart at this moment? Is it fully and completely decided? Are you prepared to change direction in order to change your story?

Write down those critical things that are critical for you to relinquish or abandon in order to change your story.

# CHAPTER 49

## CHANGING YOUR CIRCUMSTANCES

"For everyone who asks, receives. Everyone who seeks, finds.
And to everyone who knocks, the door will be opened."

**Luke 11:10 (NLT)**

$Y$our story is a reflection of your life's *circumstances*.

Those circumstances—your home environment, the places you frequent, the people with whom you spend time, the habits you develop—have changed over time. Clearly, we have no control over the early years of our lives, and those years may or may not have given your life a positive start. Some journeys start well and veer off the right path. Some start off poorly and go downhill from there.

Over time, we have much more control over our circumstances, even if we think we don't. The truth is that we have complete control over our decisions, even if those decisions are painful. One thing is very clear. If you need to change your story, you will almost certainly have to change your current circumstances. Doing so has everything to do with putting your life on a path to peace, joy, and fulfillment. At the same time, it may be the most difficult thing you ever attempt.

Old habits die hard.

Consider Mandy's story below. As you read, note the circumstances in her life and the challenges her family faced.

> *Addiction, idolatry, pride, and very worldly goals were poisoning us. It seems unreal today to think back on all the decisions and life changes we made without even spending a split second in prayer about them. Prayers were reserved for times of trouble. In October, Jerry dove head first into a life of drug addiction and alcoholism. This led to our family spending the next several months apart. This opened the door to the darkest period of our marriage.*
>
> *The more time he spent living in the world of addiction, the deeper he became trapped. I spent these months desperately*

*trying to get my husband's attention and to control his actions. I was guilty of looking to my husband for all of my hope.*

The "*world of addiction.*"

Think about that. How could her story come anywhere close to "happy" or "fulfilling" in those circumstances? Until the addiction issue is resolved, Jerry and Mandy's story only gets worse. Until they are reunited, the problems in their marriage will not improve.

It isn't difficult to know when your circumstances have gotten completely out of control; just listen to the words you use to describe them. In Mandy's story, it was "poison," "dark," and "trapped."

What words would you use to describe your story?

Those *words* have everything to do with your story, and your story cannot change without changing those words. "Dark" has to become "light," and "trapped" has to become "freedom." Those words don't change unless your circumstances change.

Remember this: *"You can't talk yourself out of problems you behave yourself into."*[51]

It is the people in your life that make up the most significant part of your life's circumstances. Quite often, those people can be the biggest part of why your story got off-track in the first place. We will take a more detailed look at those influences in the next chapter, so let's first consider these things:

- What bad (or destructive) habits in your life need to be eliminated?
- What specific situations in your life need to be avoided?
- What interpersonal conflicts or arguments in your life need to be resolved and never revisited?
- What new habits and routines do you need to develop in your life?

To actually change your story, you can't just *think* about change. You can't *wish* for change. You will have to **stop** doing those things

---

[51] Steven Covey, *The 7 Habits of Highly Effective People*. New York: Simon & Schuster, 1989. 196.

that are destructive. You will have to **leave** negative environments and replace them with positive and encouraging environments.

Yes, becoming the person that God has created you to be will require enormous change, and compromise will never work.

Paul did not mince words when he wrote his letters to the Corinthian church. "Think carefully about what is right, and *stop sinning*," he said.[52] Peter said similar things to the church as it was beginning in the first century when he forcefully admonished them to "repent of [their] sins and turn to God."[53]

It is not enough to simply *stop* what you've been doing. You must also *turn* to God.

Let's be frank with one another. Change is not easy. It requires enormous courage to do things differently, to associate with different people, and to develop new attitudes. That process is likely to continue for quite some time.

Remember, you didn't arrive where you are in a day or two, and, likewise, it will take time to change your story.

That's what Mandy discovered as her story began to change.

> *Just as God promises, He was faithful and started to work in Jerry's life. He started to hear God's voice and turned from his addiction and destructive lifestyle. As we began to rebuild our lives together, we knew that a lot of lifestyle changes were going to be necessary.*

You will have to do the same.

Changes in your circumstances, your lifestyle, are a necessary part of changing your story.

---

[52] See 1 Corinthians 15:34 (NLT).
[53] See Acts 3:19 (NLT).

# CHAPTER 50

# THOU SHALT NOT KID THYSELF

"Let no one deceive you with empty words, for because of such things God's wrath comes on those who are disobedient."

**Ephesians 5:6**

P̲oor decisions and bad choices create most of our troubles.

It makes sense, doesn't it?

Rarely, if ever, can we simply talk our way out of those troubles, but that is exactly what many people try to do. Rather than making real changes in their lives, like eliminating bad habits and replacing them with new, more productive habits, people kid themselves. They try to convince themselves, and the people around them, that it's not really that bad and that they can turn things around.

You will always be tempted to look for an easy way out of a difficult problem, but you have to look in the mirror and face reality. Changing your story means changing certain behaviors.

Participants in the popular television show, *The Biggest Loser*, learn this lesson the hard way.[54]

If you've ever watched the show, you know the participants aren't looking to take off a few extra holiday pounds. No, they are on a journey to create a completely new physical body. To do so, they often must lose well over one hundred pounds. The biggest transformation ever occurred in Season 8 of the show, when Oklahoma native Danny Cahill dropped a whopping 239 pounds!

For *Biggest Loser* contestants to create the changes they desire, it requires much more than a couple of workouts. It's not just cutting back on some calories or eliminating sugar for a couple of weeks. Instead, it takes the discipline to completely revise eating habits, to

---

[54] *The Biggest Loser*. ©2016 Universal Television LLC & Reveille LLC. *The Biggest Loser* is a trademark of Reveille LLC and its related entities.

consistently engage in challenging physical activity, and to develop a whole new attitude about physical wellness.

Many people just can't get there. In fact, it is the people who try to compromise—to bend a little rather than change completely—that fail. That is the challenge you face in changing your circumstances.

Compromise just won't work.

Read this challenge from Paul to the church in Ephesus:

> "You were taught, with regard to your former way of life, to put off your old self, which is being corrupted by its deceitful desires; to be made new in the attitude of your minds; and to put on the new self, created to be like God in true righteousness and holiness.
>
> Therefore, each of you must put off falsehood and speak truthfully to your neighbor, for we are all members of one body. "In your anger do not sin": Do not let the sun go down while you are still angry, and do not give the devil a foothold. Anyone who has been stealing must steal no longer, but must work, doing something useful with their own hands, that they may have something to share with those in need.
>
> Do not let any unwholesome talk come out of your mouths, but only what is helpful for building others up according to their needs, that it may benefit those who listen. And do not grieve the Holy Spirit of God, with whom you were sealed for the day of redemption. Get rid of all bitterness, rage and anger, brawling and slander, along with every form of malice. Be kind and compassionate to one another, forgiving each other, just as in Christ God forgave you."

**Ephesians 4:22-32**

*Get rid of your old ways*, Paul says.

There are things the people in Ephesus had to stop doing. As Paul notes, they had to "put on the *new* self."

He instructs them to replace those old, destructive habits with a new attitude and a completely different set of habits. Instead of tearing others down with unwholesome talk, the "new man" will seek to build others up. Instead of acting out of anger, rage, or pure selfishness, the "new man" will choose to act out of kindness and compassion.

It is really amazing to think about those things that Paul mentions. In truth, much of the conflict that infects our lives is a direct consequence of doing those things. Although we seek peace, joy, and happiness, how can those things arise out of lies, anger, brawling, and trash talking?

Don't kid yourself.

All it does is give the devil a foothold.

# CHAPTER 51

## THE CIRCUMSTANCES OF YOUR LIFE

> "In the paths of the wicked are snares and pitfalls, but those who would preserve their life stay far from them."

**Proverbs 22:5**

**"P**oor guy. He was just in the wrong place at the wrong time."

Have you ever heard somewhat describe something bad that happened in exactly that way? Those words, "the wrong place at the wrong time," actually make perfect sense. It describes the circumstances in which you find yourself.

The word "circumstance" originates from two Latin words: *circum* (around), and *stare* (to stand). Together, those words literally mean "that which stands around or surrounds," or the things you are standing around.[55] It implies that the current circumstances of your life are nothing more than the places and times you choose for yourself.

These are some of the most important choices you will make.

The problem is that you may feel trapped by your current circumstances. That's what Mandy said about her husband, Jerry, in the story we shared in chapter 49. She described him as being "trapped" in addiction. Part of that experience was a result of engaging in destructive behavior (doing drugs), but some of it was undoubtedly a result of being in the "wrong" place or places (influenced by his surroundings).

As you reflect on your current situation, does it sometimes feel impossible to envision a way out of the mess your life has become?

Changing your circumstances—the places you frequent, and the times you frequent them—will be an important part of reshaping your story. It is critically important for you to realize that you don't have to stay where you are.

---

[55] "circumstance, n." *Oxford English Dictionary Online*. Oxford University Press, September 2016. Web. 4 October 2016.

No matter how things appear, there is *always* a way out. Yes, we know it may not feel that way, but there are *always* people who are prepared to help you out of your current situation. Read how Jerry reacted to the terrible circumstances of his life:

> *In a huge step of faith, Jerry left his job to escape the negative influences there. God met us right where we were and walked with us every single step of the way. There are endless examples of the way the ministries of Cedar Point intervened in our lives. The men of Cedar Point surrounded Jerry and were examples of what God intended husbands to be.*

Like most working people, Jerry probably spent forty hours or more at work every week. That means he spent at least 25 percent of his life in a set of circumstances that became a serious roadblock to changing his story. Most likely, he couldn't do anything to have those people moved or replaced, so he did the only thing he could do. He left.

Jerry made a courageous decision for himself and his family, a decision that gave him the opportunity to change his story. He not only left his job, but he also replaced that set of circumstances with new ones that could heal, encourage, and support him.

To change your story, you need to evaluate your circumstances carefully. Until you find yourself "walking around" in the right places, things may *never* change. Does it make any sense whatsoever to allow God to heal your heart, but then remain in the very circumstances that have created the problems or made them worse?

Choose not to be the person in the wrong place at the wrong time.

# HeartWork Exercise No. 18

Stop for a moment and think carefully about the circumstances of your life. What words would you use to describe *your* current circumstances? Write them here:

Which of these circumstances need to change? Why?

# CHAPTER 52

# THE COMPANY YOU CHOOSE

"Do not be misled. Bad company corrupts good character."

**1 Corinthians 15:33**

God cares deeply about the people with whom you choose to surround yourself.

The reason is simple: the people you choose to spend time with influence your thinking.

Remember Jerry's experience? His circumstances at work exposed him every day to a host of negative influences that he had to escape.

It surely must not be a surprise that the people you hang around with influence your attitudes about things and impact the choices that you make. It has been said that you are the average of the five people with whom you spend the most time.[56] Of course, that is a really clever way of saying that we tend to *act like* the people with whom we spend much of our time. We tend to adopt their habits, their speech patterns, even their values.

Notice that, in the opening sentence of this chapter, we said "the people with whom you *choose* to surround yourself." No one forces our friends upon us; it is a choice we make. Quite often, it is one of the most significant choices we make in life. It was a lesson that made a huge impression on Solomon, and he shared this wisdom in the book of Proverbs:

> "Walk with the wise and become wise, for a companion
> of fools suffers harm."

**Proverbs 13:20**

If your companions are foolish—if they consistently make poor decisions that lead to problems or difficulties—then you will most

---

[56] Attributed to author and motivational speaker, Jim Rohn (1930-2009).

likely suffer right along with them. Your companions can easily lead you down a path that you need not have walked. Although you probably realize that at some level, you will often find yourself following the pack, duplicating the behavior of others in order to fit in, feel loved, or find meaning.

The point is this: God doesn't expect you to fight your battle alone, but God is very particular about who is on your team.

# CHAPTER 53

# MISGUIDED LOYALTIES

*"One who has unreliable friends soon comes to ruin, but there is a friend who sticks closer than a brother."*

**Proverbs 18:24**

The challenge in removing negative influences is that we don't want to give up on our friends. We usually feel a sense of loyalty to them, don't we?

"I can't give up my friends."

"I can't just turn my back on her."

"He needs me."

"I owe him."

Of course, loyalty is an admirable character trait. It is a critical part of creating a relationship of trust. Misguided loyalty, on the other hand, is a trap. It boxes you in and forces you to make horrible decisions.

The question is how do you know the difference? How can you identify misguided loyalty?

This is an important question because walking away from people you've long associated with can be extremely difficult. *Painfully difficult.* It can lead to huge problems within a family or within a circle of friends.

Despite this, sometimes that's exactly what needs to happen for your story to change.

If friends or family are destructive influences in the story you are trying to change, you will never be able to get on the right path until you walk away from those influences. Here is what the apostle Peter says in Scripture:

"For you have spent enough time in the past doing what pagans choose to do—living in debauchery, lust, drunkenness, orgies, carousing and detestable idolatry. *They are surprised that you do not join them* in their reckless, wild living, and they heap abuse on you. **But they will have to give account to him** who is ready to judge the living and the dead."

**1 Peter 4:3-6**

How can you know the difference between loyalty and *misguided* loyalty? Misguided loyalty occurs when you remain loyal to someone or something that is destructive to your life or prevents you from turning back to God. People who want the best for you and understand your need and desire to change your story will always encourage you. They will cheer for you. People who want the best for you won't use guilt to influence your feelings.

When someone uses guilt, a powerful form of manipulation, to keep you from giving up destructive behaviors, they are acting selfishly while, at the same time, asking you not to act in your own best interest. Think about that for a moment: "I want you to give up what's best for you so that I can get what I want from you."

Sounds pretty bad when you come out and say it, doesn't it?

> "No one else so completely sold himself to what was evil in the Lord's sight as Ahab did under the influence of his wife Jezebel."
>
> **1 Kings 21:25 (NLT)**

That's what "fools" do; they engage in activities that lead to ruin, and then encourage you to do the same. The truth is, until you walk away from them, those destructive influences will slowly erode your resolve to change your story.

Separating yourself from those influences doesn't mean you don't love them. It certainly doesn't mean that you suddenly stand in judgment of them, though they may say exactly that. No, you will find that your love for them grows significantly as you more clearly understand how deceitful Satan is. You won't see their actions as much as you see them for the person that God created them to be.

Read what Paul says about the way our lives change:

**"So we have stopped evaluating others from a**

**human point of view.** At one time we thought of Christ merely from a human point of view. How differently we know Him now! This means that anyone who belongs to Christ has become a new person. The old life is gone; a new life has begun!"

### 2 Corinthians 5:16-17 (NLT)

Changing your story is all about becoming a "new" person! Being "new" means that your perspectives have changed, your attitudes have changed, and the way you see other people has changed. You stop "evaluating others from a human point of view," as Paul says.

> "Therefore encourage one another and build each other up, just as in fact you are doing."
>
> **1 Thessalonians 5:11**

Here is what that means to you:

1. You recognize that people are flawed, just like you
2. You recognize that people desperately crave love and acceptance
3. You recognize the powerful impact of loving unconditionally
4. You recognize that people make choices about their behaviors
5. You recognize that some choices are simply foolish
6. You recognize that not everyone wants to change their behaviors

…which takes you right back to item number 1: that people are flawed, just like you are flawed.

Your choice of the people you surround yourself with is incredibly important! The wrong influences will cause you to lose sight of these six very simple principles. Some of your friends may not want to change; in fact, they may *refuse* to change. While they still need your love and encouragement, you definitely don't need that influence.

Instead, you need the positive and powerful influence of people who are prepared to love and encourage you as you change your story. Many years ago, a good friend and mentor taught one of the authors (Kelly) that everyone needs three very important people in their lives: a "Paul," a "Timothy," and a "Barnabas."

> First, a **"Paul"** in your life represents someone who serves as a spiritual mentor. A teacher. A person that can instruct you into a greater awareness and understanding of God. Someone with more experience, more wisdom, and greater insight; a special someone who can help you grow in knowledge and understanding.

> Second, a **"Timothy"** in your life represents the opposite side of the coin, a person that you are able to mentor or teach. It might be a friend or a neighbor. Someone at work or school. A teenager or a younger sibling. The idea is that learning is much more significant when we share it with someone else. Teaching others is a powerful way of staying focused on the important things we have learned. In sharing our wisdom and experiences, we "pay it forward," and grow the kingdom of God.

> Then, finally, a **"Barnabas"** in your life represents that very special friend with whom you can share anything. He or she is the person that can look you in the eye and tell you the truth without offending you or making you feel judged for having heard the truth. He or she is the person with whom you can laugh, cry, and be yourself. At the same time, neither of you are ever shy about confronting one another when necessary, knowing you are better for it.

These three people represent three very different needs in your life, people that will play important roles in your life as God changes your story.

You need all three of these people in your life.

> *Someone wise who can teach you* will help you grow and mature.

> *Someone you can teach* will ensure that others grow alongside you.

*Someone to tell you the truth* will ensure that you stay on the right path.

As you choose your influences, choose wisely.

> "Do not be unequally yoked together with unbelievers. For fellowship has righteousness with lawlessness? And what communion has light with darkness?"
>
> **2 Corinthians 6:14 (NKJV)**

# CHAPTER 54

# THE SOURCE OF ENCOURAGEMENT

*"Dear brothers and sisters, I close my letter with these last words:*
*Be joyful. Grow to maturity. Encourage each other.*
*Live in harmony and peace. Then the God of*
*love and peace will be with you."*

**2 Corinthians 13:11 (NLT)**

In Scripture, the church is described as a body.[57]

Just like every part of the body is important, every person in the church is important. Every person plays a different, yet critically important, role in the overall function of life.

Your hand, for example, is not like your foot, but both are necessary. Your ears are different than your eyes, but both are equally important.

The point is that every part of the body does something important in your life. In the same way, every individual in the church body plays a role in helping the church live and grow. The story of Nehemiah from previous chapters is a great example. Some of the people worked on rebuilding the wall while others guarded the workers; both were necessary and critical to getting the job done.

Sadly, people often have a problem with church. They may have had a bad experience (or more than one) with someone at church. They may see hypocrisy in some of the people at church. They may have felt unfairly judged. Even condemned.

> "A return to first principles in a republic is sometimes caused by the simple virtues of one man. His good example has such an influence that the good men strive to imitate him, and the wicked are ashamed to lead a life so contrary to his example."
>
> **Niccolo Machiavelli**

Is that you? Is your past experience with "church" people keeping you from the very body God designed to be your support?

---

[57] See 1 Corinthians 12:12-31 and Romans 12:4-8.

It is so important to understand that those church people are just like you. They are flawed. They often make poor decisions. The truth is that you will find flawed people everywhere, including—yes, sadly—in the church.

However, let's be clear about God's instructions to people within the church:

> "Let us hold tightly without wavering to the hope we affirm, for God can be trusted to keep his promise. Let us think of ways to motivate one another to acts of love and good works. *And let us not neglect our meeting together*, as some people do, but encourage one another, especially now that the day of his return is drawing near."

**Hebrews 10:24-25 (NLT)**

What the church needs are people who are thinking of ways to motivate one another to love and good works. You need that, too, don't you? Someone to encourage you. Someone to motivate you. That's how God designed the church to be.

The church isn't a building. It's not a set of rules and regulations. It's not even the Scriptures themselves. The church is a group of people who have recognized who Jesus Christ is and have asked Him to be the Lord of their lives. These people are identified collectively as "the church." They look to the Scripture for guidance and instruction.

So, the church can have issues because the church is made up of God's people.

Flawed people.

Forgiven people, yes, but still flawed. Each individual is somewhere on the path to maturity, but some are closer than others. Even Paul had to address church issues, meaning *people* issues:

> "Brothers and sisters, I could not address you as people who live by the Spirit but as people who are still worldly—mere infants in Christ. I gave you milk, not solid food, for you were not yet ready for it. Indeed, you are still not ready. You are still worldly. *For since*

*there is jealousy and quarreling among you, are you not world-ly?* Are you not acting like mere humans?"

**1 Corinthians 3:1-3**

Jealousy and quarreling.

People getting sideways with other people over differing opinions.

You should never let the actions of other people keep you from following God, who has promised you a life worth living. "I have come that they might have life, and have it to the full," Jesus said about His followers in John 10:10 (NLT). When your focus is on the Life-Giver, the Story-Changer, the actions of flawed people will have no control over you.

That's what Mandy and Jerry found out:

*After spending several hopeless months, I finally seemed to reach the end of my searching. God placed people around me who encouraged me to start attending church. When I regularly started attending church at Cedar Point, I began to hear God speaking into my life. Instead of spending day after day trying to manipulate Jerry's behavior, I turned him over to God, finally understanding that only He could save Jerry.*

*I began to spend all that time that I had previously wasted on worry in prayer. I was surrounded by people at Cedar Point who were encouraging and supported me.*

Embrace the body of God's people! This is what God intends.

It is the very place where God's people are called to encourage one another through the challenges of life.

You will encourage, and you will be encouraged.

You will be there for each other as God changes your stories.

# HEARTWORK EXERCISE NO. 19

It is time to take note of your influences. Take a moment and think about the people who have influenced your life. Which ones have been beneficial? Which ones do you think have been negative or hurtful?

Write down both the positive and negative influences in your life up to the present moment.

Who among your current influences do you need to remove from your life?

Who will you turn to for encouragement (be specific)?

7

# CHAPTER 55

# THE SHADOW OF FEAR

"When we arrived in Macedonia, there was no rest for us.
We faced conflict from every direction, with battles
on the outside and fear on the inside."

**2 Corinthians 7:5 (NLT)**

**A**re you afraid?

At some point in your new journey, it is possible that you may begin to waver or question yourself. After all, this is new territory.

Doubt is one thing, but *fear* is something entirely different.

Doubt is simply to be uncertain, to lack conviction. Thomas, an apostle, was not convinced that Jesus had risen from the dead. Despite the many miracles he had seen Jesus perform firsthand, it just didn't seem likely to Thomas that the Lord—savagely beaten and nailed to a cross—would arise from the grave.

> "One of the twelve disciples, Thomas (nicknamed the Twin), was not with the others when Jesus came. They told him, 'We have seen the Lord!' But he replied, 'I won't believe it unless I see the nail wounds in his hands, put my fingers into them, and place my hand into the wound in his side.'"

**John 20:24-25 (NLT)**

It's not tough to see why Thomas would struggle, is it? The physical reality that we live in simply wouldn't allow him to imagine the supernatural. That's what doubt sounds like; it's when we struggle to reconcile two conflicting ideas. It happens when what we think, what we've been told, or what we've experienced simply doesn't align with what we're asked to believe.

Fear, on the other hand, is an incredibly powerful emotion. It can literally stop you in your tracks. It can physically paralyze you. It will often prevent you from moving in a direction you would otherwise have no problem pursuing.

Fear is what Satan will use to convince you that changing your story really isn't worth the trouble. It can take on many different forms:

Fear of what other people think

Fear of loss (who or what you may have to "give up")

Fear of the unknown

Fear of being alone

Fear of failure

Fear, by definition, is something that causes you to feel threatened. It occurs when the threat of negative consequences outweighs your willingness to move forward, but that threat occurs in our minds much more often than it does in reality! We project those negative consequences because of something that *might* happen, what someone *might* think, or what we *might* lose.

On the other hand, those things might not occur at all, or the consequences may not be anywhere near as difficult as we imagine.

> "The fear of failure is the biggest single reason for failure in adult life. It is not failure itself, but the fear of failure, the prospect of failure, the anticipation of failure, that causes you to freeze up and perform at a lower level."
>
> **Brian Tracy**

Still, we imagine the very worst because Satan knows how to use that fear to manipulate you. Remember what we said way back in Chapter 4? *Satan's objective is to defeat you*, and he doesn't play fair. He doesn't want your story to change. He wants to keep you imprisoned and isolated from your Creator.

He uses your fear against you to gain control over you. He plants tiny seeds of doubt in your mind, and whispers gently in your ear:

"You'll never change."

"What are people going to think?"

"Consider what you're giving up."

"What about your friends?"

Satan wants you to dwell on the negative consequences. He wants to transform your smallest doubts into your biggest fears. He wants you to convince yourself that your decision was a mistake.

The enemy is near, as near as your shadow, and he is dangerous.

Are you afraid? If so, go immediately to that person you trust, someone outside of your circumstances that can hear and judge objectively the fears you carry. Go now and pour those fears out of your heart and into the light of day where Satan cannot use them to manipulate you.

Don't believe the lies. You *can* change your story.

# CHAPTER 56

# WHO HAS DELIVERED YOU?

"I sought the Lord, and he answered me;
he delivered me from all my fears."

**Psalm 34:4 (NIV)**

This chapter is about an entire nation that witnessed the awesome power of God first-hand, but still allowed fear to overpower them.

God delivered that nation from bondage, and the lesson is that He will do exactly the same for you!

That nation was Israel, who began as one family of about 70 people. They were all the descendants of Jacob, a man whose name God changed to Israel.[58]

Jacob's youngest son, Joseph (the one with the coat of many colors), was sold into slavery at a young age by his own brothers. Apparently, they had grown very tired of his youthful arrogance and their father's favoritism (no one else seems to have gotten a special coat). They sold him to strangers and told their father, Jacob, that he had died.

In the big scheme of things, not exactly the best start to one's life, is it?

After many years, and several twists and turns, including a stint in prison, Joseph ultimately becomes very important and very powerful. By God's hand, Joseph eventually rules the nation of Egypt, answering only to Pharaoh himself![59]

Back in Joseph's homeland, his father and family experience a great famine. Threatened with starvation, Jacob learns that Egypt has food to spare.

---

[58] See Genesis 32:28.
[59] The entire story of Joseph is found in Genesis 37-50. In chapter 41, you can read how Pharaoh makes him the ruler of Egypt.

"When Jacob heard that grain was available in Egypt, he said to his sons, 'Why are you standing around looking at one another? I have heard there is grain in Egypt. Go down there, and buy enough grain to keep us alive. Otherwise we'll die.' So Joseph's ten older brothers went down to Egypt to buy grain."

**Exodus 32:1-3 (NLT)**

The brothers, however, soon learn that Joseph is now the governor of Egypt and responsible for selling the nation's grain. Imagine his brothers' reaction when they are confronted with the fact that little brother is basically running the country!

Shock. Disbelief. Fear. Guilt, followed by even more fear. *What will Joseph do to us?* However, the biggest surprise is yet to come:

"But don't be upset, and don't be angry with yourselves for selling me to this place. It was God who sent me here ahead of you to preserve your lives. This famine that has ravaged the land for two years will last five more years, and there will be neither plowing nor harvesting. God has sent me ahead of you to keep you and your families alive and to preserve many survivors. So it was God who sent me here, not you!"

**Genesis 45:5-8 (NLT)**

Say what?

Joseph has the perfect opportunity, the absolute *perfect* payback, and he takes a pass?

It is an incredible story. Could you possibly see things the way Joseph did? "It was God who sent me here," Joseph says. No, nothing to do with his brothers. It was God's plan all along.

The story of Joseph is a powerful story of faith and forgiveness, and, most importantly, a story that demonstrates the power of God to dramatically change any story.

OK, so why is this story important to this chapter? *Well, we're getting there…*

Once the family is reunited with Joseph, they stay in Egypt with him. And, over time, the family prospers and grows in numbers, while Joseph's relationship with the Egyptian Pharaoh provides the protection they need to live in that foreign land.

However, both Joseph and Pharaoh eventually die, and the sheer numbers of the Israelites become a threat to the new Pharaoh. Worried that these "foreigners" might join with the enemies of Egypt and overthrow them, the new Pharaoh enslaves the Israelites. He works them mercilessly. It is a very dark period of time for the Israelites. At one point, to prevent further growth of the nation of Israel, Pharaoh declares that every newborn Israelite boy will be killed.

It is at this point that the Israelites cry out to God for deliverance. And God responds. He appears to Moses, an Israelite himself who had grown up in a royal Egyptian household.[60] God gives Moses the task of leading the Israelites out of Egyptian bondage into a land he had long ago promised to the descendants of Jacob.

> "Then the Lord told [Moses], 'I have certainly seen the oppression of my people in Egypt. I have heard their cries of distress because of their harsh slave drivers. Yes, I am aware of their suffering. So I have come down to rescue them from the power of the Egyptians and lead them out of Egypt into their own fertile and spacious land....
>
> Look! The cry of the people of Israel has reached me, and I have seen how harshly the Egyptians abuse them. Now go, for I am sending you to Pharaoh. You must lead my people Israel out of Egypt.'"

**Exodus 3:7-10 (NLT)**

Moses, through the power of God, leads the Israelites out of Egypt! Just imagine the joy and relief of freedom!

After years of oppression and slavery and hopelessness, the Israelites pack up their belongings and hit the road. They must have thought that it would be SO easy now! Moses beat the Pharaoh of Egypt! Our worries are over!

Or so they thought. First, Pharaoh has a change of heart. No

---

[60] See Exodus 3:7-10.

sooner does he allow the Israelites to leave than he decides he made a mistake. He orders his entire army out to bring the Israelites back to Egypt.

Thus it happens that, as the nation of Israel approaches the Red Sea, they find their way forward blocked by the swollen river and the Egyptian army rapidly approaching from the rear. And fear raises its ugly head:

> "As Pharaoh approached, the people of Israel looked up and panicked when they saw the Egyptians overtaking them. They cried out to the Lord, and they said to Moses, 'Why did you bring us out here to die in the wilderness? Weren't there enough graves for us in Egypt? What have you done to us? Why did you make us leave Egypt? Didn't we tell you this would happen while we were still in Egypt? We said, 'Leave us alone! Let us be slaves to the Egyptians. It's better to be a slave in Egypt than a corpse in the wilderness!'"

**Exodus 14:10-12 (NLT)**

That quickly, the people move from joy and elation to fear and blame.

Still, God is faithful. A promise is a promise! Once again, He miraculously rescues Israel.

Surely, the Israelites must now be convinced. First, God performs miracles in Egypt, and now the parting of the Red Sea saves them from Pharaoh's army. Surely, after witnessing God's awesome power, the people will have the confidence to overcome any adversity. But, unfortunately, they do not. Reaching the wilderness barely one month after leaving Egypt, the Israelites are at it yet again:

> "There, too, the whole community of Israel complained about Moses and Aaron.
>
> 'If only the Lord had killed us back in Egypt,' they moaned. 'There we sat around pots filled with meat and ate all the bread we wanted. But now you have brought us into this wilderness to starve us all to death.'"

**Exodus 16:2-3 (NLT)**

The Israelites are ready to turn right around and head back to a life of slavery and oppression in Egypt. Evidently, the people still cannot see that God will provide for all of their needs. But, once again, God does exactly that. This time He delivers all the food the Israelites could possibly need and more.

On the outside, looking in, it's hard to imagine that people could so easily forget and so easily give up, especially after seeing God's power at work. After all, God had answered their prayers and delivered them from slavery. God had delivered them from certain death at the Red Sea!

That's human nature. And Satan knows it.

No matter how God's power may be working in your life, Satan is not content. He is not about to give up. Over and over again, the Israelites overlooked the awesome power of God's hand and succumbed to doubt and fear.

What can you learn? Although you have been rescued from your previous life, you are still vulnerable. Despite the fact that you have witnessed God's power to heal your heart and radically change your story, you may still doubt.

Do you doubt? Are you fearful?

***Who has delivered you?***

# CHAPTER 57

# YOU'VE BEEN GIVEN EVERYTHING YOU NEED

*"David also said to Solomon his son, 'Be strong and courageous, and do the work. Do not be afraid or discouraged, for the Lord God, my God, is with you....'"*

**1 Chronicles 28:20**

**"A**re *you going to be one of those religious nuts?"*

Have you suddenly been confronted with the reality that not everyone is as excited about your new journey as you are? When someone you know feels uncomfortable with the changes in your life—perhaps because they feel ashamed or threatened, or they may even think that you're judging them for staying where they are—they may begin to take potshots at you.

Hopefully not, but the chances are decent that someone may be threatened by your radical change in direction. Yes, there will be some people who rejoice with you and encourage you, but there may be others who will be reminded of their own problems and their own insecurities. Instead of encouraging you, they may want to drag you back into the fray.

*"It will never last."*

*"You're not good enough."*

*"You can't do it."*

The truth is, when someone says things like this, it is often nothing more than their own fears talking. Losing you, or confronting the reality of their own lives, can cause others to say and do things that are hurtful to you.

This can be a very vulnerable time in your journey. You may doubt your strength or ability. It's important for you to realize that God has not only changed your story, but He has also given you a road map for the journey!

"His divine power has given us **everything we need** for a godly life through our knowledge of him who called us by his own glory and goodness. Through these he has given us his very great and precious promises, so that through them you may participate in the divine nature, having escaped the corruption in the world caused by evil desires.

For this very reason, **make every effort to add to your faith** goodness; and to goodness, knowledge; and to knowledge, self-control; and to self-control, perseverance; and to perseverance, godliness; and to godliness, mutual affection; and to mutual affection, love. For if you possess these qualities in increasing measure, they will keep you from being ineffective and unproductive in your knowledge of our Lord Jesus Christ."

**2 Peter 1:3-8**

Peter tells us that God has given us everything we need.

Let that sink in for a moment.

*Everything you need.*

Here are seven very important things He has provided through His Son, Jesus:

1. **Abundant life**
   "I came that they may have life and have it abundantly." (John 10:10 RSV)

2. **Salvation**
   "For I am not ashamed of this Good News about Christ. It is the power of God at work, saving everyone who believes...." (Romans 1:16 NLT)

3. **A new heart**
   "And I will give you a new heart, and I will put a new spirit in you." (Ezekiel 36:26)

4. **Wisdom**
   "If you need wisdom, ask our generous God, and he will give it to you." (James 1:5 NLT)

5. **His Spirit**

   "Don't you realize that all of you together are the temple of God and that the Spirit of God lives in you?" (1 Corinthians 3:16 NLT)

6. **Rest**

   "Come to me, all you who are weary and burdened, and I will give you rest." (Matthew 11:28)

7. **Peace**

   "And the peace of God, which transcends all understanding, will guard your hearts and your minds in Christ Jesus." (Philippians 4:7)

It's like you're leaving on a very long journey, and someone has just given you two completely full suitcases with all the essentials for your trip. Of course, you still have to travel, but you have everything you need to start the journey. And the best part is that inside one of the suitcases is a map and a guidebook!

You must *"make every effort,"* Peter says, to use that guidebook to learn and grow. This means, of course, that you have work to do!

It starts with changing some behaviors (seeking moral excellence) and continues with putting God's word into your heart and mind. Then, you can work on self-control, patience, and right living. And love.

When you think about it, your journey is exactly like the story of the Israelites' exodus from Egypt we shared in chapter 48. Like them, you have been rescued, and, like them, you are now on a journey to the Promised Land.

Like the Israelites on their journey out of Egypt, you will encounter difficulties along the way.

Be courageous! You have everything you need.

# HEARTWORK EXERCISE NO. 20

It is normal to have doubts, but how do you respond to those doubts?

Some people will get anxious to the point of inaction. Others will allow doubt to devolve into their worst fears. The point is that Satan loves to step into that environment and use those doubts to manipulate you.

It is always helpful to remember the future state that you are striving for, and to compare it to the present challenge that you have to face. For example, you intend to change your story to avoid the pain and bitterness you have experienced, but a friend you have known for years is highly critical of you in public. Your fear is what other people will think or that they might treat you differently. It's keeping you up at night and filling you with despair.

Consider the future. Yes, it will be a challenge in the short term, but allowing God to fill you with hope and courage gives you "the power to face a disagreeable present in the interest of desirable permanent ends."[61] That is how courage is defined: not as the absence of fear, but as the ability to persevere in spite of your doubts and fears.

Yes, some friends may desert you. A family member may ridicule you. A co-worker may try to intimidate you. Still, the future is bright...your story is changing!

Be strong and courageous.

Are you experiencing doubts of any kind? If so, write them down.

---

[61] William DeWitt Hyde. "The Cardinal Virtues." *The Atlantic Monthly* (Volume 88, Page 116). Houghton Mifflin and Company (1901).

# CHAPTER 58

## THE BIG LIE

> "It teaches us to say 'No' to ungodliness and worldly passions,
> and to live self-controlled, upright and godly
> lives in this present age."
>
> **Titus 2:12**

**P**raise God! Your story is changing!

You, dear brother or sister, are rebuilding the walls of your life. God has come alongside you and given you hope and courage as you've begun to change your direction, your circumstances, and your influences.

Though doubts and fears have threatened, you have found your way!

However, let's not forget that Satan is still trying to grab a foothold in your life. Sadly, Satan will continue to look for any weakness he might exploit. At this point, one of the biggest challenges in your walk with God might be the idea that life just won't be as fun as it used to be.

Yes, Satan loves that lie.

Here you are. You are overjoyed! You are ecstatic about changing your story. Escaping all the pain of your former life was the best thing that could've happened to you, but now...

Now.

Now, what?

You look back on the "other side" and see people in the world enjoying the "good things" in life, prospering, and having so much...fun. You may begin to wonder if you've traded one unfulfilling lifestyle for a different one.

Sometimes, let's face it, the world looks pretty appealing.

Of course it does. That's exactly what Satan wants to do—make sin look desirable.

Here is an old fable that describes exactly what we mean:

> One day, while walking down the street, a highly successful executive was hit by a bus, and he died. His soul arrived up in heaven where he was met at the Pearly Gates by St. Peter himself. "Welcome to Heaven," said St. Peter. "Before you get settled in though, it seems we have a problem. You see, strangely enough, we're not exactly sure what to do with you."
>
> "No problem," said the man. "Just let me in."
>
> "Well, I'd like to, but we need to sort things out," St. Peter replied. "So, what we're going to do is let you spend one day in Hell and one day in Heaven, and then you can choose the one in which you would like to spend eternity."
>
> "Well, actually, I think I've made up my mind," the man insisted. "I prefer to stay in Heaven!"
>
> "Sorry," said St. Peter. "We have rules." And, with that, St. Peter put the man in an elevator and sent it down, down, down to hell.
>
> The doors opened and the man stepped out onto a lush, beautiful golf course. In the distance was a country club, and standing right in front of him were all his friends—fellow executives that he had worked with, all dressed in suits and cheering for him. They ran up, shook his hand, and began talking about the good old days. Later, they played a fabulous round of golf, followed by an excellent lobster dinner at the club. He also met the Devil who, as it turns out, seemed to be a nice guy.
>
> The man was having such a good time that before he knew it, it was time to leave. So, he took the elevator back up to the Pearly Gates and found St. Peter waiting for him. "Now it's time to spend a day in heaven," St Peter said.

The man spent the next 24 hours lounging around on clouds, playing the harp, and singing. He had a wonderful time, and before he knew it the 24 hours were up and St. Peter came to get him.

"So, you've spent a day in hell and you've spent a day in heaven. Now you must choose your eternity," he said. The man paused for a second. Then, haltingly, he said, "Well, I never thought I'd say this. I mean, heaven has been really great, but I think I had more fun in hell."

So, St. Peter escorted him to the elevator and again he went down, down, down to Hell.

When the doors of the elevator opened, the man found himself standing in a desolate wasteland covered in garbage and filth. He saw his friends dressed in rags, picking up garbage and putting it in sacks.

The Devil came up to him and put his arm around him. "I don't understand," stammered the man. "Yesterday, I was here, and there was a golf course and a country club. We ate lobster, and we had a great time. Now, everything I see is awful, and the people look miserable."

The Devil looked at him and smiled.

*"Yesterday we were recruiting you. Today, you're on the staff."*

It might be funny were it not so true.

Satan's ploy is to tempt you with the idea that you're "missing out." He shows you the pleasures of sin, but conveniently hides the consequences—and the consequences of sin are extreme.

"For the wages of sin is death, but the gift of God is eternal life in Christ Jesus our Lord."

**Romans 6:23**

Of course the world looks appealing! What Satan shows you is the "fun."

What he doesn't show you is the misery, the addiction, the jealousies, the fear, or the conflict. The mistake is in thinking that joy in life is somehow tied to material possessions or self-indulgence.

The bigger lie is that you can't have real fun as a Christian, that somehow you're missing out on the things that really bring happiness.

You know that's a lie, don't you?

You've already suffered through that lie.

# CHAPTER 59

# THE ENVY OF PROSPERITY

> "Praise be to the God and Father of our Lord Jesus Christ,
> who has blessed us in the heavenly realms with
> every spiritual blessing in Christ."

**Ephesians 1:3**

$S$atan will do anything to separate you from God.

He will use any trick, any device, anything possible to drive a wedge between you and the one who has changed your story.

That's why the love of money, for example, is a problem.

> "For the love of money is a root of all kinds of evil. Some people, eager for money, have wandered from the faith and pierced themselves with many griefs."

**1 Timothy 6:10**

Notice that money itself is not the problem; it's the *love* of money. It can cause people to make terrible choices in their lives.

Something that is just as bad, and probably akin to the love of money, is the envy we may experience of other people who have money or things. That problem can become an incurable cancer in your life if you don't defeat it completely.

David himself had to deal with those feelings.

We have talked a lot about David in this book. Clearly, he was an extraordinary man, yet, as we have discovered, in many ways he was completely ordinary.

The difference, of course, is that David was a man totally and completely given to God. The well-known 23rd Psalm provides all the insight you need to understand David's devotion:

> "The Lord is my shepherd; **I have all that I need**.
>
> He lets me rest in green meadows; he leads me beside

peaceful streams. He renews my strength. He guides me along right paths, bringing honor to his name.

Even when I walk through the darkest valley, **I will not be afraid**, for you are close beside me. Your rod and your staff protect and comfort me.

You prepare a feast for me in the presence of my enemies. You honor me by anointing my head with oil. My cup overflows with blessings. Surely your goodness and unfailing love will pursue me all the days of my life, and I will live in the house of the Lord forever."

**Psalm 23 (NLT)**

*I have all I need.*

*I will not be afraid.*

David echoes those thoughts over and over as he reveals who God is in his life in the book of Psalms.

"The Lord is my rock, my fortress and my deliverer; my God is my rock, in whom I take refuge, my shield and the horn of my salvation, my stronghold."

**Psalm 18:2**

*God is my rock. My refuge. My stronghold.*

Despite this faith, listen to David describe a challenge he faced in his journey:

"But as for me, I almost lost my footing. My feet were slipping, and I was almost gone.

**For I envied the proud when I saw them prosper despite their wickedness.** They seem to live such painless lives; their bodies are so healthy and strong. They don't have troubles like other people; they're not plagued with problems like everyone else.

They wear pride like a jeweled necklace and clothe themselves with cruelty. These fat cats have everything their hearts could ever wish for! They scoff and speak only evil; in their pride they seek to crush others. They boast against the very heavens, and their words strut throughout the earth. And so the people are dismayed and confused, drinking in all their words.

'What does God know?' they ask. 'Does the Most High even know what's happening?' **Look at these wicked people—enjoying a life of ease while their riches multiply. Did I keep my heart pure for nothing?** Did I keep myself innocent for no reason? I get nothing but trouble all day long; every morning brings me pain. If I had really spoken this way to others, I would have been a traitor to your people.

**So I tried to understand why the wicked prosper. But what a difficult task it is!**

Then I went into your sanctuary, O God, and I finally understood the destiny of the wicked. Truly, you put them on a slippery path and send them sliding over the cliff to destruction. In an instant they are destroyed, completely swept away by terrors. When you arise, O Lord, you will laugh at their silly ideas as a person laughs at dreams in the morning.

*Then I realized that my heart was bitter,* and I was all torn up inside. I was so foolish and ignorant—I must have seemed like a senseless animal to you. Yet I still belong to you; you hold my right hand. You guide me with your counsel, leading me to a glorious destiny.

Whom have I in heaven but you? I desire you more than anything on earth. My health may fail, and my spirit may grow weak, but **God remains the strength of my heart; he is mine forever.**"

**Psalm 73:2-26 (NLT)**

Yes, even David, the mighty warrior King, struggled to understand how people can forsake God, do evil in the world, and still prosper.

Look at how angry he was: *"Look at these wicked people—enjoying a life of ease while their riches multiply. Did I keep my heart pure for nothing?"*

Then, he realized that it was his heart that was bitter.

This is exactly what Satan will do in your life. He wants you to look at the people around you and compare yourself to them. He wants you to become jealous of what you see. He wants you to believe they are blissfully happy and content, that life presents no difficulties for them. He wants you focused on what you do *not* have instead of the blessings that you experience.

As you know from some of the stories in this book, this is completely deceiving. True happiness is not found in possessions. Although there is certainly nothing wrong with money or possessions, you can go completely astray if you *love and serve* those things.

Again, Satan will do anything to separate you from God.

And what could possibly be more appealing than to show you a world that revels in prosperity as they follow their own selfish paths?

# CHAPTER 60

# THE THINGS YOU CAN'T BUY

*"But Peter replied, 'May your money be destroyed with you for thinking God's gift can be bought!'"*

**Acts 8:20 (NLT)**

**G**od's blessings are, first and foremost, the things that money simply *cannot* buy.

Money cannot buy peace.

It cannot buy you love.

It certainly won't buy you joy.

These are the things that most people would give any amount of money to have—once they come to the realization that their money won't provide them.

As famed motivational speaker Zig Ziglar often said, "The things you have that money *won't* buy are the things that will enable you to get more of the things that money *will* buy."

Remember when we talked about happiness back in chapter 32? Without question, God's greatest joy is that you will be happy! Not later, but now! God and Satan are on opposite sides of the fence when it comes to defining happiness. Satan defines it as something you experience in a moment; God defines it as a state of being.

> "To the person who pleases him, **God gives wisdom, knowledge and happiness,** but to the sinner he gives the task of gathering and storing up wealth to hand it over to the one who pleases God. This too is meaningless, a chasing after the wind."

> **Ecclesiastes 2:26**

No, God doesn't take a moment in your life, a mere experience, and call it happiness. Instead, He provides happiness as an integral part of your life. That true happiness comes from knowing a loving

God that cares about you. It comes from the assurance that God will never leave you.

> "Keep your lives free from the love of money, and be content with what you have because God has said, 'Never will I leave you; never will I forsake you.'"

**Hebrews 13:5**

Happiness is when, despite your circumstances, you know and experience real love, the kind of love that comes from an expression of caring without any expectations whatsoever.

It is awe-inspiring to think that someone would do something significant for you, even sacrificial, for no reason—no personal gain, no glory, no payment in return.

Christ did exactly that. He did something that money could *never* buy.

That selfless act has provided you with an opportunity to completely change your story!

> "You see, at just the right time, when we were still powerless, Christ died for the ungodly. Very rarely will anyone die for a righteous person, though for a good person someone might possibly dare to die. But God demonstrates his own love for us in this: While we were still sinners, Christ died for us."
>
> **Romans 5:6-8**

# HeartWork Exercise No. 21

The blessing of happiness is experienced most fully when you experience the joy of helping and serving others. It is that work that forces you to think of others and their needs, and savor the joy you create in helping them in some way.

Jesus gave us that example. In John 13, Jesus provided this final lesson to his disciples when He, the King of kings, took a towel and a bucket of water and washed their feet. Keep in mind that, in those days, the roads were dusty and people wore sandals. No pavement. No hiking boots.

Imagine those feet! Imagine the Son of God stooping to such a lowly act.

> "After washing their feet, he put on his robe again and sat down and asked, 'Do you understand what I was doing? You call me "Teacher" and "Lord," and you are right, because that's what I am. And since I, your Lord and Teacher, have washed your feet, you ought to wash each other's feet. I have given you an example to follow. **Do as I have done to you.**'"

**John 13:12-15 (NLT)**

Whose feet do you need to wash?

No, not literally, of course, but to whom can you provide comfort? Who can you help? In whose life can you be a blessing?

Write those names down below:

# PART V

# A REFLECTION OF THE HEART

"As water reflects a face,
so a man's heart reflects the man."

**Proverbs 27:19**

"It is only with the heart that one can
see rightly what is essential is invisible to the eye."

**Antoine de Saint-Exupery**

# CHAPTER 61

# THE HUMBLE HEART

"'My hands have made both heaven and earth; they and everything in them are mine. I, the Lord, have spoken! I will bless those who have humble and contrite hearts, who tremble at my word.'"

**Isaiah 66:2 (NLT)**

*In chapters 61-64, we will look at four primary characteristics of a heart that reflects the presence of God in one's life.*

The first reflection of a Godly heart is **humility**.

When you hear that word, your first tendency may be to think of someone who doesn't brag about her accomplishments, for example, or someone who doesn't assert his opinion.

Real humility is to defer to someone else, allowing them to be more significant than you for some specific reason. It is an acknowledgement that someone else is more important. It is to willingly consider someone else's needs as more important than your own.

That is what God speaks of when He speaks of humility. Godly humility is to be obedient to the will of God *because* He is God. It is to consider His commands and His judgments to be more important than our own *because* He is the Creator.

It is, in fact, to be just like Jesus:

> "Who, being in very nature God, did not consider equality with God something to be used to his own advantage; rather, he made himself nothing by taking the very nature of a servant, being made in human likeness. And being found in appearance as a man, he humbled himself by becoming obedient to death—even death on a cross!"

**Philippians 2:6-8 (NLT)**

You see, Jesus was God in the flesh. If *anyone* could have asserted his rights, demonstrated his power, or gotten what he desired, Jesus would have been that person. Instead, in deference to God's plan, Jesus not only set those "rights" aside, but He willingly gave His life for the sins of the world.

For Christians, a humble heart is one that, first of all, acknowledges that God is creator of the universe. Secondly, it is a heart that acknowledges the saving power of the sacrifice of Jesus. When a Christian truly believes those two things, he or she cannot help but be humble.

What does that mean to you in practical, everyday terms? It means that you have a heart that is willing to set aside the need to *be* right and replace it with the need to *do* right just because of your love for Jesus.

> "Who is wise and understanding among you? Let them show it by their good life, by deeds done in the humility that comes from wisdom."

**James 3:13**

Perhaps one of the biggest areas in which we face challenges with being humble is within our family relationships, particularly within our marriages. Most often, it is a lack of humility—the inability to set aside our own selfish demands—that leads to so many broken marriages.

> "Husbands, love your wives, just as Christ loved the church and gave himself up for her."
>
> **Ephesians 5:25**

It is our pride, or selfishness, that can transform a small, meaningless disagreement into something much more significant than it should be. It happens to all of us. The truth is that we often value "being right" far more than we value the relationship itself!

Read, in the words of one of the authors (Rick), a poignant story from his life:

*It was one of those times.*

*I would like to think that every married couple has them. My wife and I had just had a disagreement, an argument, really. Some would call it a "fight."*

*I was in a room with the door shut and the TV turned up almost as loud as it would go. She was in the kitchen, hurt and angry. She was putting dishes away and slamming doors to make sure I understood that she was still upset about the conversation that had taken place.*

*As I sat there in my recliner, frustrated and justifying my actions, there arose a momentary thought of humility, that I should go and apologize. "Tell her you're sorry and ask her to forgive you," I thought.*

*But I quickly brushed that idea aside. "I am always apologizing," I thought, "and she never does." Besides, I clearly wasn't wrong.*

*So, I sat there for a few more minutes, stewing. That thought returned, but again I refused. In fact, I had taken a firm stance against any act of accepting blame or responsibility for the conflict that had just taken place.*

*So, what was the fight about? Surely it must have been a pretty big deal for me to take such a hard stance, right? Frankly, I don't remember. I really have no clue whatsoever.*

*I will never forget what happened next. Once again, I thought that I should apologize, and, once again, I argued with myself. This time, I had another thought come to me. Over time, I've come to call these kind of thoughts "God thoughts" because they are not the kinds of thoughts you would usually have. In fact, it was a thought that would actually be contrary to what someone might typically think in moments like that.*

*This came to me: "You think you are hardening your heart towards your wife, don't you?"*

*"Absolutely. If she thinks I'm going to apologize, then she's wrong," I thought. Then, this came to me: "she's not the one telling you to apologize right now. I am."*

*Suddenly, every ounce of my justification slipped away. Any morsel of self-righteousness or any refusal to take on a role that I perceived as martyrdom in my marriage left me. The whole time it was God who was dealing with me. It was the Holy Spirit prompting me to make things right. He was trying to teach me that WHAT is right trumps WHO is right every time.*

*More importantly, the lesson to me was that preserving my relationship with my wife was far more important than holding my ground on something that had absolutely no eternal significance.*

It is just so easy for us to harden our hearts, isn't it? How many times have we felt wronged and felt the need to "balance the scales"?

That is why humility can be so difficult. It takes the influence of God for us to consider our relationships more important than winning an argument or proving a point, as Rick learned:

*That night, the Lord taught me that the only way I could harden my heart towards my wife was if I first hardened my heart towards Him. It is one of the most valuable lessons I have ever learned.*

*I still look back on that moment and wonder what my life would be like now had the Lord not been able to get my attention. What if I had allowed the voice of my self-justification to drown out the gentle prompting of the Holy Spirit?*

From the outside, looking in with no emotional attachment, it is a bit easier to see what was happening. That selfish thought was really Satan's attempt to deceive, to harden Rick's heart to God's working in his life. That deception would have had a negative effect, not only on that moment, but it may have created a lasting effect on his entire marriage and the rest of his life!

> "He has shown you, O mortal, what is good. And what does the Lord require of you? To act justly and to love mercy and to walk humbly with your God."
> **Micah 6:8**

The point is that, without humility, we would never really care about pursuing anyone's interests other than our own. We would only care about being right, getting even, or feeling justified in our positions and our behaviors.

Forgiveness is a direct extension of our humility. It is an acknowledgement that without God's forgiveness we would be completely lost.

"In prayer there is a connection between what God does and what you do. *You can't get forgiveness from God, for instance, without also forgiving others.* If you refuse to do your part, you cut yourself off from God's part."

### Matthew 6:15 (MSG)

Have you ever hardened your heart to God's dealing with you, all the while totally unaware that it was *God* dealing with you?

Humility allows your heart to be open to the prompting of God's spirit.

It is also what allows you to forgive, and to ask forgiveness, without feeling that you are less of a person for having done so.

> "Bear with each other and forgive one another if any of you has a grievance against someone. Forgive as the Lord forgave you."
>
> **Colossians 3:13**

# CHAPTER 62

# THE COMMITTED HEART

"For the eyes of the Lord range throughout the earth to strengthen those whose hearts are fully committed to him."

**2 Chronicles 16:9**

*In chapters 61 to 64, we are looking at four primary characteristics of a heart that reflects the presence of God in one's life.*

The second reflection of a Godly heart is **commitment**.

God doesn't just want a part of you.

He doesn't want the New Year's resolution version of you that gives up after a couple of weeks. He doesn't want the Christmas and Easter version of you that makes a cameo appearance twice a year. He doesn't want the Sunday-only version of you. He certainly doesn't want the "hot one day and cold the next" version of you.

> "So, because you are lukewarm—neither hot nor cold—I am about to spit you out of my mouth."
>
> **Revelation 3:16**

He wants *all* of you, 100 percent of you.

In the New Testament, when Jesus asked people to follow Him, He didn't ask for part-timers or temporary workers. He told His disciples that being a Christ-follower required *serious* reflection:

> "Then he said to the crowd, 'If any of you wants to be my follower, you must give up your own way, *take up your cross daily*, and follow me. If you try to hang on to your life, you will lose it. But if you give up your life for my sake, you will save it. And what do you benefit if you gain the whole world but are yourself lost or destroyed?'"
>
> **Luke 9:23-25 (NLT)**

Not surprisingly, it's the same thing that Moses said to the Israelites back in the Old Testament after God had rescued the nation from slavery in Egypt:

> "And you must love the Lord your God with all your heart, all your soul, and all your strength. **And you must commit yourselves wholeheartedly** to these commands that I am giving you today."

**Deuteronomy 6:5-6 (NLT)**

Following Jesus is about committing your heart to Him. Changing your story is not as simple as checking a few boxes, or going to church once in a while, or giving up a bad habit. Following Jesus is about making Him both Lord and Savior of your life. The part that most people struggle with is not the "Savior" part of that equation; it's the "Lord" part.

Making Jesus the Lord of your life means that you've committed yourself to serving Him, obeying His will, and keeping His commands. In fact, the Greek word for commitment literally means to put yourself into the hands of another.[62]

Even though your mind may be *convinced* that following Jesus is story-changing, it is not until your heart is *convicted* that your life will be transformed and your story will truly change.

One of the great illustrations of commitment in Scripture is found in the story of Elisha. As a young man, Elisha was asked by the prophet Elijah to become his assistant, and eventually Elisha would become a prophet of God himself.

> "So Elijah went and found Elisha son of Shaphat plowing a field. There were twelve teams of oxen in the field, and Elisha was plowing with the twelfth team. Elijah went over to him and threw his cloak across his shoulders and then walked away. Elisha left the oxen standing there, ran after Elijah, and said to him, 'First let me go and kiss my father and mother good-bye, and then I will go with you!' Elijah replied, 'Go on back, but think about what I have done to you.'

---

[62] The Greek word for commitment is *paradidomi*.

So Elisha returned to his oxen and slaughtered them. He used the wood from the plow to build a fire to roast their flesh. He passed around the meat to the towns-people, and they all ate. Then he went with Elijah as his assistant."

**1 Kings 19:19-21 NLT**

Elisha did not leave himself with any options. He did not have a "Plan B."

His livelihood was earned using his oxen to plow fields. He not only slaughtered those animals for food, but he also used the wood from the plow to build the fire!

He was all in. There was literally no way to go back to his former life.

That is what a committed heart looks like. It forgets the sins of the past and dedicates itself to a new path.

Remember, commitment is a decision.

It is a decision you make first in your mind, and then make *complete* in your heart.

> "I don't mean to say that I have already achieved these things or that I have already reached perfection. But I press on to possess that perfection for which Christ Jesus first possessed me. No, dear brothers and sisters, I have not achieved it, but I focus on this one thing: Forgetting the past and **looking forward to what lies ahead, I press on to reach the end of the race** and receive the heavenly prize for which God, through Christ Jesus, is calling us."
>
> **Philippians 3:12-14 NLT**

# CHAPTER 63

# THE UNDIVIDED HEART

*"Teach me your way, O Lord, and I will walk in your truth; give me an undivided heart, that I may fear your name."*

**Psalm 86:11**

*In chapters 61 to 64, we are looking at four primary characteristics of a heart that reflects the presence of God in one's life.*

The third reflection of a Godly heart is **unity**.

God wants you to have a heart that is *not divided*, a heart that is given *only* to God and those things that He has determined is good.

God did not create your heart to be divided. He created it to have a single intent. It is what David referred to as a "pure" heart.[63] The simple understanding of an undivided heart is that you cannot pursue both good and evil at the same time. You cannot desire both right and wrong simultaneously.

It's one or the other. The Scripture describes it this way:

> "No one can serve two masters. For you will hate one and love the other; you will be devoted to one and despise the other. You cannot serve both God and money."

**Matthew 6:24 NLT**

You cannot serve God and something else at the same time. Making money is one thing; *serving* money—making it your God—is quite another thing.

What can easily happen, as David discovered in his life, is that you can be momentarily deceived by Satan. You can choose selfishly, thinking, for example, that your temporary happiness is actually better for you than what God has declared is best for you. Quite often, these momentary lapses in judgment have disastrous consequences.

---

[63] See Psalms 51:10.

It's why David prayed fervently in Psalm 86, asking God to give him an *undivided* heart.

It's why he pleaded with God in Psalm 51 to give him a *pure* heart.

Having experienced the pain and consequences of poor choices in the past, David desperately wanted to avoid making the same mistake again. He knew that only God could keep his heart pure and undivided.

The truth is, when we lose sight of God, we become susceptible to deceit. It's like being hopelessly lost in the wilderness and realizing that you have no compass. With nothing to guide you, you have no idea which way to go or which decision is best.

To keep this from happening in your life, you simply cannot afford to lose sight of God's Word. His Word is your compass; His Word is what you need to live the life you thought only others lived, but not *you*.

> "For the Lord grants wisdom! From his mouth come knowledge and understanding. He grants a treasure of common sense to the honest. He is a shield to those who walk with integrity. He guards the paths of the just and protects those who are faithful to him.
>
> Then you will understand what is right, just, and fair, and you will find the right way to go. **For wisdom will enter your heart, and knowledge will fill you with joy. Wise choices will watch over you.** Understanding will keep you safe."

**Proverbs 2:6-11 (NLT)**

Creating the habits of prayer and Bible study are critical to keeping your heart undivided, but creating new habits can be a challenge!

In the New Testament, Paul writes two letters to a young preacher named Timothy. In the first letter, he tells Timothy something very important:

> "Have nothing to do with godless myths and old wives' tales; rather, **train yourself to be godly**. For

physical training is of some value, but *godliness* has value for all things."

**1 Timothy 4:7-8**

Paul tells Timothy to *train* himself to be Godly. It is fascinating that that the original word that is translated in that passage as "training" (the Greek word "gumnasio") is the same word from which we derive the English word "gymnasium." Paul was prescribing a spiritual workout!

What might that training look like?

It's not unlike what you would do in the gym. You start at a certain level, and, as you get in better shape, you slowly add on more weight, or more miles, or more workouts. Spiritually speaking, you begin with your faith in Jesus as the beginning level. Then, you begin to "add" to your faith as you grow:

Peter described that process this way:

> "For this very reason, make every effort to add to your faith goodness; and to goodness, knowledge; and to knowledge, self-control; and to self-control, perseverance; and to perseverance, godliness; and to godliness, mutual affection; and to mutual affection, love. For if you possess these qualities in increasing measure, they will keep you from being ineffective and unproductive in your knowledge of our Lord Jesus Christ."

**2 Peter 1:5-8 (NLT)**

Notice that the first thing to add to your faith is goodness, a word that means "virtue" or "moral excellence." You practice those actions (those virtues) that God has determined are good, virtues that include actions like serving others, providing help for those in need, and giving comfort and encouragement to those in distress.

Notice that the very next thing that Peter said that must be added to our faith is knowledge. It is growing in the understanding of the will of God as provided for us in the Bible.

"Make every effort," Peter says. It means that these things are continually in your thoughts. It means that you are striving consistently to become what God created you to be.

Continue to train!

Pray continually for God to give you an undivided heart.

Read the Word consistently so that you may grow in your knowledge of God.

# CHAPTER 64

# A LOVING HEART

"Sow righteousness for yourselves, reap the fruit of unfailing love, and break up your unplowed ground; for it is time to seek the Lord, until he comes and showers his righteousness on you."

**Hosea 10:12**

*In chapters 61 to 64, we are looking at four primary characteristics of a heart that reflects the presence of God in one's life.*

The fourth reflection of the Godly heart is **love**.

We know that it is humility that causes us to consider the interests of others as important as our own, but it is the presence of God's love (agape) that causes us to act on our faith in Jesus. In his letter to the Galatian church, Paul put it in the simplest of terms:

> "The only thing that counts is faith expressing itself through love."

**Galatians 5:6**

Think about what Paul has said. The very essence of mending your heart and changing your story is to express your gratitude for those things by loving others. As Jesus has changed your life, He wants you to create a lasting impact on others by allowing them to see that change in your life!

Paul consistently prayed that we would grow in His love:

> "And this is my prayer: **that your love may abound more and more in knowledge and depth of insight,** so that you may be able to discern what is best and may be pure and blameless for the day of Christ, filled with the fruit of righteousness that comes through Jesus Christ—to the glory and praise of God."

**Philippians 1:9-11**

How important is it that God's working in your life causes you to love others? Read what Paul wrote to the church at Corinth:

> "If I could speak all the languages of earth and of angels, **but didn't love others**, I would only be a noisy gong or a clanging cymbal. If I had the gift of prophecy, and if I understood all of God's secret plans and possessed all knowledge, and if I had such faith that I could move mountains, **but didn't love others**, I would be nothing. If I gave everything I have to the poor and even sacrificed my body, I could boast about it; **but if I didn't love others**, I would have gained nothing."

**1 Corinthians 13:1-3 (NLT)**

According to Paul, you might speak every language, tell the future, understand everything there is to know about God, and give away everything you have; however, if you couldn't genuinely LOVE (agape) others, then all that would amount to nothing.

Nothing.

Christianity is not an event on Sunday. It's not being seen to be religious. It's not even knowing a lot about the Bible. The only thing that demonstrates your right relationship with Jesus is your willingness to act, to give of yourself to others out of love for Jesus. In fact, that is the very reason God has put you on this earth.

> "For we are God's handiwork, *created in Christ Jesus to do good works*, which God prepared in advance for us to do."

**Ephesians 2:10**

Why would you do those things unless you have completely grasped the magnitude of what Jesus has done for you?

> "This is how we know what love is: Jesus Christ laid down his life for us. And we ought to lay down our lives for our brothers and sisters."

**1 John 3:16**

Notice, then, the progression of the four reflections of the Godly heart.

- <u>Humility</u>: the acknowledgement of who God is and what He has done, leading us to forgive others as He forgave us

- <u>Commitment</u>: the unwavering conviction to be, and to do, what God has called you to be and do

- <u>Unity</u>: the vigilant and prayerful pursuit of a pure and undivided heart, so that we are not deterred or deceived by Satan

- <u>Love</u>: the ultimate expression of faith; to do good for others in a way that mirrors the love that Jesus has for us

So, you see, your story is directly related to these four reflections of the heart.

The heart that is transformed cannot help but be humble before God.

The heart that is transformed can see no other path except God's path.

The heart that is transformed is focused on staying that way.

The heart that is transformed has a love for their new life that cannot be contained.

As David said, "one's life reflects the heart."[64]

---

[64] See Proverbs 27:19.

# HeartWork Exercise No. 22

For a moment, let's imagine that we are having a discussion about your life one year from today. We are sitting across from one another, reminiscing about the past twelve months and reflecting on your progress over the past year. In your mind, what would have happened during that time for you to *know* that your heart had been healed and your story had changed?

Write those things down below:

Now, think about the challenges that are present in your life right now. What challenges do you need to overcome to make the things you listed above happen for you?

Write those things down below:

# CHAPTER 65

# WHAT HAS THE LORD PUT IN *YOUR* HEART?

> "I had not told anyone what my God
> had put in my heart to do...."
> **Nehemiah 2:12**

**W**hat an amazing journey this has been!

As you look back on where you've been and what you've learned, our prayer is that you have placed your faith completely in Jesus and His story-changing message.

> "We know what real love is because Jesus gave up his life for us. So we also ought to give up our lives for our brothers and sisters. If someone has enough money to live well and sees a brother or sister in need but shows no compassion – how can God's love be in that person? Dear children, let's not merely say that we love each other; let us show the truth by our actions."

**1 John 3:16-18 (NLT)**

The message of Jesus is to love and to help others. It is that love and concern that gives people a reason to have hope in their own lives. Make no mistake; God will use your life and your experience to impact the hearts of others!

The only question is "How?"

Throughout this book, we have shared many stories of real people whose stories have been changed. They were rescued by the Master Story-Changer, Jesus, and they found real love, real joy, and real peace.

No, they didn't find perfection. Nor did they find that life suddenly had no challenges. What they did find was purpose, comfort, and value. Here is how Andrew talks about that discovery:

*I entered into this new life with nothing but an invitation. I walked out of my home with no money, no job, no car, and no idea what I was going to do. I only knew, with every fiber of my being, that I had to respond to that red-letter invitation of, "Follow me."*

*This is the longest I've been clean and sober since the age of twelve. The first time I've truly felt free, wanted, and worth something. I may not be rich, but I'm happy. I may not be popular, but I have a family. I may not be wise, but I'm learning. I don't have much, but I'm not lacking. I'm not making leaps and bounds, but I'm not standing still. I'm not in heaven yet, but I'm definitely not at rock bottom anymore.*

*I want to thank those from both then and now. Thank you for love and support. Thank you for not giving up, even when I already had.*

*Above all, I thank God. When I deserved (and wanted) nothing but death, He gave me life. When I was enveloped by darkness, He showed me the light. When I was at my very lowest, He brought me to the highest. When I was at my weakest, He gave me my strength. When I was falling apart, He put me together. When I finally let go of all that I had, He gave me all that I needed.*

### Excerpt from Andrew's story

Hope and happiness. With those things comes a life worth living, an abundant life.

Make no mistake, God will use your life, and your influence, and your story, to impact someone else!

Remember Nehemiah? When he was serving as cupbearer to the king thousands of miles from Jerusalem, the knowledge that his home city was still in shambles placed an enormous burden on his heart. In tears, he purposed to return to Jerusalem and to lead the people of that once great city to rebuild its walls.

God placed that burden on Nehemiah's heart. God knew that a certain kind of man, a certain kind of leader, was needed to complete that difficult task. He knew that the perfect individual for the job would be someone who was passionate about the city of Jerusalem.

That person was Nehemiah.

So, here you are. No matter what your background may be, no matter what your past may look like, no matter what challenges you have experienced, there is a place where God needs you.

He might need you exactly where you are. He might need you to help a specific person. He might need you to get involved in a project somewhere else. He might need you to take on a leadership role. Whatever your talent is, and wherever your passion may lie, God knows.

You need not worry; God will make your purpose clear.

Your mission is to continue to prepare your heart for the works He has prepared in advance for you to do.[65]

Now, what will God put in your heart to do?

> "Commit to the Lord whatever you do, and he will establish your plans."
>
> **Proverbs 19:21**

---

[65] See Ephesians 2:10.

# PART VI

# GOD'S INSTRUCTIONS

"And now I'm changed.
And now I'm stronger."

***Something in the Water***
*(Written by Chris DeStefano, Brett James, and Carrie Underwood)*

"Therefore, anyone who rejects this instruction
does not reject a human being, but God,
the very God who gives you his Holy Spirit."

**1 Thessalonians 4:8**

# CHAPTER 66

# GOD'S INSTRUCTIONS FOR BEING SAVED

> "This is good, and pleases God our Savior, who wants all people to be saved and to come to a knowledge of the truth...."
>
> **1 Timothy 2:3-4**

**B**ecoming a Christ-follower—inviting Jesus to be the Lord of your life—is the most important decision that you will make. It will set the foundation for all of your relationships and provide the means for living a joyful and victorious life! Most importantly, it will connect you intimately with your Creator and provide ultimate purpose for your life.

In this chapter, we have outlined God's instructions for becoming a Christian, but it is important to note that being a Christ-follower is not a singular event—it is a way of living. You don't just *become* a Christian; you *are* a Christian.

Paul explains in 2 Corinthians 5:17 (NLT): "This means that anyone who belongs to Christ has become a new person. The old life is gone; a new life has begun!"

Here is how you get started in that new life:

First, you must believe in the death, burial, and resurrection of Jesus. In his letter to the Corinthian church, the apostle Paul laid out the fundamentals of the gospel message, the foundation of why followers place their hope and trust in Jesus:

> "Now, brothers and sisters, I want to remind you of the gospel I preached to you, which you received and on which you have taken your stand. By this gospel you are saved, if you hold firmly to the word I preached to you. Otherwise, you have believed in vain.
>
> For what I received I passed on to you as of first importance: that Christ died for our sins according to the Scriptures, that he was buried, that he was raised

on the third day according to the Scriptures, and that he appeared to Cephas, and then to the Twelve. After that, he appeared to more than five hundred of the brothers and sisters at the same time...."

**1 Corinthians 15:1-6**

Paul said that if you believe that message, and if you confess that belief before men, your *faith* will save you.

"If you declare with your mouth, 'Jesus is Lord,' and *believe in your heart* that God raised him from the dead, you will be saved. For it is with your heart that you believe and are justified, and it is with your mouth that you profess your faith and are saved."

**Romans 10:9-10**

Believing "in your heart," as Paul says, is the beginning of your faith, a word that simply means trust. Faith is a trust that causes you to believe and then to act on that belief. It is faith that causes you to transfer control of your life into God's hands—because you believe that He is real, and because you are convinced that He will fulfill the promises He has made to you:

"And without faith it is impossible to please God, because anyone who comes to him must believe that he exists and that he rewards those who earnestly seek him."

**Hebrews 11:6**

Note that faith is not simply a mental exercise (believing He exists); it is active obedience to the commands of Jesus (earnestly seeking Him). It is in that obedience, a response based in love, that you demonstrate your faith:

"If you love me, *keep my commands*. And I will ask the Father, and he will give you another advocate to help you and be with you forever—the Spirit of truth. The world cannot accept him, because it neither sees him nor knows him. But you know him, for he lives with you and will be in you."

**John 14:15-17**

This is the most exciting aspect of giving your life to Jesus. When you choose to love and obey Him, God gives you His Holy Spirit to guide and comfort you. Read the message of the apostle, Peter, delivered shortly after the resurrection of Jesus:

> "Fellow Israelites, I can tell you confidently that the patriarch David died and was buried, and his tomb is here to this day. But he was a prophet and knew that God had promised him on oath that he would place one of his descendants on his throne. Seeing what was to come, he spoke of the resurrection of the Messiah, that he was not abandoned to the realm of the dead, nor did his body see decay. *God has raised this Jesus to life, and we are all witnesses of it.* Exalted to the right hand of God, he has received from the Father the promised Holy Spirit and has poured out what you now see and hear."

**Acts 2:29-33**

> "Therefore let all Israel be assured of this: God has made this Jesus, whom you crucified, both Lord and Messiah."
>
> When the people heard this, they were cut to the heart and said to Peter and the other apostles, 'Brothers, what shall we do?'
>
> Peter replied, 'Repent and be baptized, every one of you, in the name of Jesus Christ for the forgiveness of your sins. And you will receive the gift of the Holy Spirit.'"

**Acts 2:36-38**

When they believed the message (they were "cut to the heart"), they asked what they should do. Peter's response was that they should act on their trust by turning from their old life of sin and be baptized (immersed in a symbolic grave to "die" to their old ways). At the moment of baptism, God provides you with the gift of the Holy Spirit.

The truth is that your decision to obey God is the same decision Jesus made when He obeyed the will of God, the Father.

"And being found in appearance as a man, [Jesus] humbled himself by becoming obedient to death— even death on a cross."

**Philippians 2:8**

Becoming a Christian is, therefore, a simple process:

1. Believe passionately in the life of Jesus and the sacrifice He made in order to restore your relationship to God, the Father. (Faith)

2. Turn away from your old way of life, in which you acted on your own selfish desires, and turn to Jesus. (Repentance)

3. Confess your belief in the death, burial, and resurrection of Jesus.

4. Die to yourself. This is what "baptism" is—a burial in water (mimicking the death and resurrection of Jesus) and a proclamation that you are no longer your own and that you have surrendered to the Master Story-Changer.

5. Walk with Jesus daily, obeying His commands. "But if we walk in the light, as he is in the light, we have fellowship with one another, and the blood of Jesus, his son, purifies us from all sin (1 John 1:7)." (Continuing in your faith)

These are the fundamentals of making Jesus your Lord and Savior.

There is, of course, much more in the Bible about the way Christians live, conduct themselves, and spread the gospel message, but this is how you begin your "new life" with Jesus.

# CHAPTER 67

# GOD'S INSTRUCTIONS FOR RIGHT LIVING

"No, O people, the Lord has told you what is good, and this is what he requires of you: to do what is right, to love mercy, and to walk humbly with your God."

**Micah 6:8 (NLT)**

**O**nce you have changed your story and created a whole different path for your journey, God expects you to see life very differently. He also expects you to see other people very differently!

First, Jesus provides Christians with a "new command:"

"A new command I give you: Love one another. As I have loved you, so you must love one another."

**John 13:34**

Before Jesus, the Law prescribed that we would love each other as we love ourselves.[66] Now, He commands that we would raise the bar considerably and love each other as He loved us, remembering that He gave His life on our behalf!

Next, in his letter to the church in Galatia, Paul shared the "law" of Christ:

"Carry each other's burdens, and in this way you will fulfill the law of Christ."

**Galatians 6:2**

Demonstrating our love for each other, a command of God, and carrying each other's burdens, the law of Christ, are the two pillars of right living as God has prescribed it. The New Testament writers gave us plenty of detail as to the specifics of bringing those principles into our lives.

In his letter to the church at Colossae, Paul provides these instructions:

---

[66] See Romans 13:9.

"Therefore, as God's chosen people, holy and dearly loved, clothe yourselves with compassion, kindness, humility, gentleness and patience. Bear with each other and forgive one another if any of you has a grievance against someone. Forgive as the Lord forgave you. And over all these virtues put on love, which binds them all together in perfect unity."

**Colossians 3:12-14**

He also discusses these principles in his letter to the church in Ephesus:

"Therefore, each of you must put off falsehood and speak truthfully to your neighbor, for we are all members of one body. 'In your anger do not sin': Do not let the sun go down while you are still angry, and do not give the devil a foothold. Anyone who has been stealing must steal no longer, but must work, doing something useful with their own hands, that they may have something to share with those in need.

Do not let any unwholesome talk come out of your mouths, but only what is helpful for building others up according to their needs, that it may benefit those who listen. And do not grieve the Holy Spirit of God, with whom you were sealed for the day of redemption. Get rid of all bitterness, rage and anger, brawling and slander, along with every form of malice. Be kind and compassionate to one another, forgiving each other, just as in Christ God forgave you."

**Ephesians 4:25-32**

Right living is uniquely opposed to "being right." The idea of being right is to act out of selfish interests, or to get what you think *you* deserve. Living rightly, on the other hand, is the process of reflecting the spirit of God in your everyday interactions with others and treating them as Jesus would have treated them.

Finally, in his letter to the church in Rome, Paul added these detailed instructions on right living:

"Be devoted to one another in love. Honor one another above yourselves. Never be lacking in zeal, but keep your spiritual fervor, serving the Lord. Be joyful in hope, patient in affliction, faithful in prayer. Share with the Lord's people who are in need. Practice hospitality.

Bless those who persecute you; bless and do not curse. Rejoice with those who rejoice; mourn with those who mourn. Live in harmony with one another. Do not be proud, but be willing to associate with people of low position. Do not be conceited.

Do not repay anyone evil for evil. Be careful to do what is right in the eyes of everyone. If it is possible, as far as it depends on you, live at peace with everyone."

**Romans 12:10-18**

These are high standards for our lives, but when we are convinced that Jesus is who He says He is—the Son of God, who willingly gave His life that we might live—then we cannot help but live, and love, as He did.

As Paul says, "...Christ's love compels us."[67]

---

[67] See 2 Corinthians 5:14.

## RICK BURKE, SENIOR PASTOR

Rick is the senior pastor at Cedar Point Church.

In 2006, after 17 years as Youth Pastor at Faith Christian Family Church in Clovis, New Mexico, Rick returned to his hometown of Claremore, Oklahoma—a small community northeast of Tulsa best known as the home of humorist and entertainer, Will Rogers—and began work as pastor of Cedar Point, a small church of about 65 people.

As pastor, Rick has been dedicated to three simple ideas: building relationships, being relentlessly good to the community, and sharing his faith in the Master Story-Changer, Jesus Christ. Over the past ten years, Cedar Point has grown to over 1,000 members and four worship services.

Rick is married to Tina, and together they have three children and two grandchildren (with another on the way!). For more information, visit **www.cedarpointchurchonline.com**.

## KELLY RIGGS

Kelly is the founder and president of Business LockerRoom, Inc., a consulting firm located in Broken Arrow, OK. He is an author, a speaker, and a business performance coach for individuals and companies throughout the United States.

Kelly is also very involved in ministry, serving over the past 25 years as a deacon, adult Bible class teacher, and visiting preacher. Kelly is married to Rhonda, and together they have three children and two grandchildren (with another on the way!). For more information, visit **www.kellyriggs.com**.